THE TIMES
GOING UNDERGROUND

LONDON
BY TUBE

Matthew Tanner & Joss Waterfall

navigator guides

Published by Navigator Guides
www.navigatorguides.com

Published by Navigator Guides
The Old Post Office, Swanton Novers,
Melton Constable, Norfolk NR24 2AJ
www.navigatorguides.com
info@navigatorguides.com

**A catalogue record for this book is available
from the British Library.**

The publishers have made every effort to ensure
the accuracy of information in the book at the
time of going to press. However, they cannot
accept responsibility for any loss, injury or
inconvenience resulting from the use of
information contained in this guide.

All photographs by Joss Waterfall © Navigator
Guides Ltd except for pages 15,20,23,72,77,87,
106,123,131,153 and 171 © Antonia Cunningham
Cover photograph © Horacio Monteverde
Inside back map © PC Graphics (UK) Ltd
Colour reproduction PDQ Digital Media
Printed in Italy by Printer Trento srl

Publisher: Rupert Wheeler
Managing Editor: Antonia Cunningham
Editor: Susannah Wight
Cover Design: Horacio Monteverde
Typeset in The Sans and Mittleschrift

CONTENTS

INTRODUCTION

The Tube makes London simple. Even for people who live here, it can be a vast, frantic, bewildering place. Yet all of its sights, pubs, restaurants and bars, as well as cinemas, theatres and endless shopping opportunities, are easily accessible once you venture underground. Exploring London by Tube means not getting lost, avoiding traffic jams, getting to your destination quickly and, with a Travelcard, roaming at will.

The Underground is an historic achievement that has shaped the capital. This guide treats the network as an attraction in its own right. If you head off to London's Transport Museum (*see* p.156), best reached by going to Covent Garden Tube on the Picadilly line (3 mins), you can learn about its fascinating history.

If you find yourself suffering from Tube fatigue, spare a thought for the two men who stopped at all 275 Tube stations on the London Underground network in 2004, to finish in a world record-breaking time of 18 hours, 35 minutes and 43 seconds!

The Underground Map

The first all-inclusive map of the London Underground was published in 1906. With the routes traced over an ordinary map, it served its purpose up to a point but was hard to understand. Harry Beck, a 29-year-old unemployed engineering draughtsman, saw that it could be improved and, in his own time, sketched out in an exercise book the basis of what became a design classic.

Inspired by his work drawing electrical circuits, Beck's design broke with a traditional map format and limited routes to horizontal, vertical and 45-degree diagonal lines. All surface detail, except for a simplified version of the River Thames, was omitted and each of the lines, although they were already colour-coded, was given a more distinctive colour to make the map easier to read, especially at night. Perhaps most importantly, he made the central area (now Zone 1) out of proportion to its size, as if

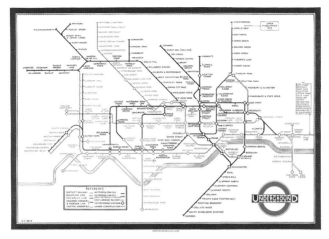

seen through a convex lens, and shrank the
outlying areas so that the entire network
could be concentrated into a manageable
format.

Although London Transport rejected the
design in 1931 as too 'revolutionary', Beck was
more successful a year later and a trial map
was printed in 1933. The travelling public
took to it from the start and a version of the
map has been in use ever since.

Sadly for Beck, he had signed away his
copyright for a pittance in 1937. Since then,
the map has been through several revisions
but it still clearly shows its debt to Beck with
the design proving itself flexible enough to
accommodate many changes in the system.
A room at the London Transport Museum
(*see* p.156) has now been named after Beck
to honour the man who brought clarity
and ease of use to the most complicated
underground rail network in the world.

HOW TO USE THIS BOOK

This book is as easy to navigate as London
is by Tube. Each section is devoted to a one
line: Bakerloo, Central, Circle, Jubilee,
Northern, Piccadilly and Victoria. **There are
no separate sections for the Hammersmith
& City or the Metropolitan lines, because
these both run in tandem with part of the
Circle line.** The Circle and District lines are

combined because they stop at the same stations. Taken together, the lines in this book service every major Tube stop in London Underground's central Zone 1, which has something of interest close by. There is also a chapter called Further Afield (*see* p.176), if you have more time and wish to visit places outside of Zone 1 on the Tube.

Organization

- Under each stop, the sights above ground are listed in order of walking time from the station.

- Where appropriate, sights are organized in a straightforward walking route.

- Where attractions are in a different direction, one direction is followed first before returning to the station and following the sights in another direction. You will be aware that this has happened when an attraction has a shorter walking time than the entry that precedes it.

- The first two pages of each section act as a contents list for the Underground line in question and show you the order of stations (either going north to south or east to west) as well as the places you can visit at each station.

- If a station is an intersection between lines, attractions may be described in a section for another line and there will be a page reference for you to find the entry. These are marked, *see* p.oo.

- Stations that are intersection stations and service more than one line are indicated with coloured squares that relate to the colours of each line on the Underground map and are shown on page iii.

- These line contents start with the first Underground station on the line that has a listing and continue to the last one that has a listing, including all the stations in between, whether they have a listing or not.

- Only the stations that have a listing are shown in the rest of the section.

Gabriel's Wharf *see* p.99

The line or route you take is a matter of choice or convenience. If you have an attraction in mind, consult the index on p.188 and it will direct you to the entry and the station that you need. Then look at the Tube map on the inside front cover of this book to see the best way to get there. Alternatively, you may want to explore a single line. On the Central line, for example, you could travel from west to east, to visit Portobello Market and Notting Hill (Notting Hill Gate) in the morning, have lunch in one of the many eateries in Selfridges (Bond Street), and then have an afternoon in the Wallace Collection admiring French and Dutch masters. Or you might line hop and switch from the Central line to the Bakerloo line at Oxford Circus for a stroll through Regent's Park. Finally, if the weather is good, why not take the Jubilee line and head for Gabriel's Wharf (Southwark) to enjoy a pizza and a bottle of wine beside the river? Whatever you want to see or do in London, it's easy by Tube. This guide provides a key.

Maps and Information

In conjunction with using this guide, visitors should arm themselves with a good map. You can get one from any tourist information booth. The best source of information is Transport for London's Tube website (www.tube.tfl.gov.uk), where you'll find maps (www.map.tfl.gov.uk/map is very useful), details of tickets and station facilities, as well as up-to-date information about delays or problems. The Journey Planner gives you transport options, journey times and prices between any two points in London.

HMS Belfast see p.120

Note that if you are only travelling for one station, your destination will usually be within less than a 10-minute walk. Also, that for the purposes of this book, lines and stations have been chosen for each sight, but that other lines and stations may also be appropriate.

Restaurants and Cafés
Recommendations for lunchtime cafés and restaurants are listed for many of the stations. You will never be more than a short walk or two Tube stops away.

Inexpensive	under £15
Moderate	£15–30
Expensive	more than £30

Opening Times
All opening times are given in the text. Note that most places are shut on 24/25th December and 1st January, as well as other public holidays. Please call or check the website for opening hours at these times.

TUBE INFORMATION

Tickets
Tickets are available from any Tube station; 1-day, 3-day and 7-day travelcards can also be bought at London Travel Information Centres, National Rail stations and local London Transport ticket outlets. Under-5s travel free, there are concessions for children aged 5–15 (see below). **Please note, these prices were valid when this book went to press in 2005; they increase annually.**

Single fares

Zone 1	Adult £2	Child 60p
Zone 1 & 2	Adult £2.30	Child 80p

Carnet

A book of 10 single Underground tickets.

Zone 1 only	Adult £17	Child £5

1-day Travelcards

Off-peak cards are valid for Zones 1–2, Mon–Fri after 9.30am and any time at the weekend or public holidays on Tube, rail and bus.

Zones 1–2	Adult £4.70	Child n/a
Zones 1–6	Adult £6	Child £2

Family Travelcards

One-day tickets for up to two adults and four children. Groups need not be related but must travel together at all times. Children aged 14–15 require a photocard (*see* below). Tickets valid Mon–Fri after 9.30am and any time at the weekend or public holidays. Children go free Sat–Sun.

Zones 1–2	Adult £3.10	Child 80p
Zones 1–6	Adult £4	Child 80p

7-day and Pre-pay Oyster Cards

Oyster cards can be used as a 7-day (or more) Travelcard or as a pay-as-you-go card where you put money on the card and spend it as you travel. For both types, fares are cheaper than standard single tickets and will never add up to more than a 1-day Travelcard for the furthest zone you have used. Use Pre-pay before 9.30 and fares are more expensive. You may be charged £3 for the Pay-as-you-go card, but return it to a ticket office before you leave London and you will be refunded.

Zones 1–2	Adult £21.40	Child £8.60
Zones 1–6	Adult £39.50	Child £17.20

London Underground Tourist Vouchers

If your travel agent offers you London Underground tourist vouchers before you come refuse them as they are more expensive than buying tickets on site...

Photocards
These are required for Travelcards for seven
days or longer and by 14- and 15-year-olds
buying child tickets. Photocards are free. Take
a passport-sized photo to any Underground
station, London Travel Information Centre
of local London Transport outlet. Child
Photocards require proof of age and a
completed application form.

Access for wheelchair users
Currently, only some Underground stations
are not dependant on steps for access but,
although progress may seem slow, there
are plans for 70 stations to have wheelchair
access over the next 15–20 years. The new
Jubilee line extension from Westminster to
Stratford has lifts at all its stations and
new trains on the Jubilee and Northern
lines have areas designed for wheelchairs,
colour-contrasted handrails and audio and
visual systems that announce destination
information and the name of each station.

Transport for London has produced an
Underground map for wheelchair users and
mobility impaired people. This map show
the accessibility of station entrance and exit
points, access details when changing from
one line to another and the height of the
step from the platform to the train.

For more details and a copy of the map,
telephone: (020) 7222 1234.

For more information about accessibility
to London's sights and hotels, visit the
Greater London Access and Disability
website at www.glad.org.uk.

Lost Property
If you think you've lost something in a
Tube station or on a Tube within the last 48
hours, return to the station and ask staff in
person. If it's more than two days since you
lost an item, call the Lost Property Office
(*see* below) or make an online enquiry.

London Transport Lost Property Office
200 Baker Street, NW1
Tel: 0845 330 9882; www.tfl.gov.uk
Open: Mon–Fri 8.30am–2pm, closed bank hols

The Millenium Bridge
see p.98

Toilets

The following stations have gents' and ladies' toilets on site, in mainline stations or nearby (you must have a valid ticket to use toilets in a 'compulsory ticket area'): Baker Street, Canary Wharf, Euston, Farringdon, King's Cross/St Pancras, Liverpool Street, London Bridge, Marylebone, Paddington, Piccadilly Circus, South Kensington, Victoria, Waterloo, Westminster.

Tube etiquette and safety

For the comfort and safety of everyone using the Tube, there are a few easy rules that you should follow:

- When on escalators, stand on the right so that people who want to walk up or down can pass you on the left.
- When you get on the train, move away from the doors so that there is space for other people to get on.
- Plan your route so you can move through the station easily. Do not stop at the bottom of stairs if there are people behind you.
- Always keep all your luggage with you
- If you can, avoid travelling with luggage at peak times.
- Do not eat smelly food on the Tube.
- It is forbidden to smoke anywhere on the Tube or in the Tube station.
- As a safety precaution, there are no litter bins on the Underground network so please take your litter with you.
- Be alert for any unattended bags. If you see something that looks suspicious, contact the nearest LU staff member.

The Sherlock Holmes Museum

BAKERLOO LINE

The Bakerloo Line was originally financed by an American, Charles Tyson Yerkes. The name 'Bakerloo' was an appropriation of the 'Baker Street and Waterloo Railway', and was coined by a newspaper — much to the chagrin of certain contemporary railway journals, who called it a 'gutter title'. Rumour has it that the idea for the line originated from a few London businessmen who wanted to get to Lord's Cricket Ground as quickly as possible. The Bakerloo Line was the first to cross London from north to south, and opened in 1906. At first it was not entirely successful, but extensions to its initial three-mile length were made in 1917 as far as Watford; by 1939 it went to the Elephant and Castle; and only in 1989 did it extend to Harrow and Wealdstone.

MARYLEBONE

Lord's Cricket Ground (15 mins)

St John's Wood Rd (ticket office Grove End Road),
***Tel**: (020) 7432 1033 or 7289 1611; www.lords.org*
***Open**: Museum open for spectators on match
days with tickets, or entry included in guided
tour;* ***Adm**: adults £2.50, concessions £1*
***Guided tours** (except during major matches and
preparation days): Apr–Sep daily, 10am, noon
and 2pm, Oct–Mar daily, noon and 2pm; adults
£7, concessions £5.50, children £4.50, family £20*
Gift shop; Wheelchair accessible

Headquarters of English cricket, the
Marylebone Cricket Club is not a place to
come with naïve questions about overs,
innings and lbw. Highlights of the small
museum include the Ashes, the terracotta
trophy contested in matches between
England and Australia (actually the remains
of a bail burnt by the supporters of the
Australian side after being beaten by the
MCC in 1883); and a sparrow – now stuffed –
which was killed by a particularly vicious
delivery here in 1936. While touring the
ground you can't miss the futuristic and
architecturally acclaimed Media Centre,
which stands on the northeast side like a
large white spaceship.

BAKER ST

Madame Tussaud's and the London Auditorium (2 mins)

Marylebone Road, NW1
***Tel**: 0870 400 3000*
www.madame-tussauds.co.uk
***Open**: Mon–Fri 8.30am–5.30pm, Sat–Sun
9am–6pm*
***Adm**: adults £21.99, child £16.99, concessions
£17.99; under-5s free; adm slightly reduced if
arrive later in day and reduced by £2 if you do
not wish to see the 'Chamber Live'; buy tickets
in advance online or by phone, as queues can
be up to 2 hrs long*
*Gift shop, cafés; Wheelchair accessible
(phone ahead)*

Love it or hate it, Madame Tussaud's is the
third most visited attraction in London

**Seashell Fish
Restaurant K6**

49–51 Lisson Grove

*Tel: (020) 7724 9000;
www.seashell
restaurant.co.uk*

*Open: Mon–Fri
noon–2.30 and
5–10.30, Sat
noon–10.30pm*

*Takeaway Inexpensive
Restaurant Moderate*

Great fish and chips
in a café-style
setting, or you can
take it away.

Madame Tussaud's and the London Auditorium

topped only by the British Museum and the National Gallery. It first opened its doors in 1802 when Madame Tussaud, a former drawing mistress of King Louis XVI's children, came to England fleeing the French Revolution with her collection of death masks. Although their power is today less intense, they still hold a weird fascination.

Madame Tussaud's has several sections. In the first exhibit, *Blush*, themed around a celebrity party, you'll find the bottom-wiggling Kylie and pole-dancing, chest-heaving Britney, and Madonna reclining demurely on a *chaise longue*. In fact, bottoms seem more the theme since you are encouraged to consider the merits and squeezability of all – Brad Pitt included. *Premiere Night* is where you can rub shoulders with the likes of Pierce Brosnan as 007, Harrison Ford as Indiana Jones and Marilyn Monroe. In the *World Stage* you come face-to-face with royalty, politicians, dictators, writers and more assorted celebrities.

In the basement is the *Chamber of Horrors*, where Dr Crippen and Jack the Ripper stare back at you and the blade that chopped off Marie Antoinette's head is gruesomely on display. A separate room, *Chamber Live*, exhibits escaped prison inmates (live actors) who attempt to frighten you out of your wits (with appropriate warnings for visitors). Finally, the *Spirit of London* carries you in a London taxi through 400 years, from Elizabethan times to the present day.

Next door, the *Show Dome*, offers two shows: 'Warriors' illustrates a battle between Alexander the Great and Achilles using a combination of live action and technology; 'Journey to Infinity' takes you on a celestial journey through our solar system past comets, planets and moons, asteroid belts and exploding supernovas. After the show you can visit the Show Dome's museum where there are waxworks of pioneering astronauts Neil Armstrong and 'Buzz' Aldrin, live satellite broadcasts from space and a machine to gauge how much you'd weigh if you were on the moon.

Quiet Revolution N6

62–64 Weymouth St; tube Baker St, Bond St

Tel: (020) 7487 5683

Open: Mon–Sat 9am–6pm

Inexpensive

An organic café in a modern interior, serving snacks, sandwiches and soups.

Pâtisserie Valerie at Sagne

105 Marylebone High St

Tel: (020) 7935 6240; www.patisserie-valerie.co.uk

Open: Mon–Fri 7.30am–7pm, Sat 8am–7pm, Sun 9am–6pm

Inexpensive

Mouthwatering snacks and cakes in this famous French patisserie.

The Sherlock Holmes Museum

Sherlock Holmes Museum (3 mins)

239 Baker St (from Marylebone Road, turn right)
Tel: *(020) 7935 8866; www.sherlock-holmes.co.uk*
Open: *daily 9.30am–6pm*
Adm: *adults £6, children £4*
Gift shop; No facilities for wheelchair users

221b Baker Street (though actually it's number 239) is the home of the fictional sleuth Sherlock Holmes, where you are greeted by a Victorian policeman and escorted round the house by Holmes's housekeeper, Mrs Hudson. Created according to hints and descriptions from the stories of Conan Doyle, the rooms are very convincing, and contain, of course, the detective's famous magnifying glass, pipe and deerstalker hat.

REGENT'S PARK

Regent's Park

Regent's Park (2 mins)
Park Information Office: Store Yard, Inner Circle
***Tel**: (020) 7486 7905; www.royalparks.gov.uk*
***Open**: daily 5am–dusk; **Adm**: free*
***Open air theatre**: summer only; **Tel**: 08700 601811; www.openairtheatre.org*

Originally part of Middlesex Forest and then a royal hunting ground, Regent's Park was laid out from 1817 to 1828 by the architect John Nash. One of London's neatest parks, its rose gardens within the inner circle are pristine with beds of colourful flowers that bloom in profusion throughout the summer. There are plenty of attractions: rowing on the lake, which is also home to herons and black swans (open Apr–Sep Mon–Fri 10am–5pm, Sat–Sun and hols 9am–7pm, weather permitting; adults £4/hr, children £2/hr, pedalos £2/15 mins; there's a smaller pond for children's boating); six cafés; three playgrounds; a bandstand for music; and tennis courts. In the delightful Queen Mary's Gardens, you'll find impressive gardens and an open-air theatre, which has daytime and evening performances – a perfect excursion for balmy summer evenings.

London Zoo (20 mins)
Outer Circle, Regent's Park (north side: walk up the Broad Walk and turn left on the Outer Circle)
***Tel**: (020) 7722 3333; www.londonzoo.co.uk*
***Open**: summer daily 10am–6pm, winter 10am–4pm*
***Adm**: adults £13, concessions £11, 3–15s £9.75, family £41; 10% off online bookings*
Daily events (see the website)
Cafés, snack bars, gift shop; Wheelchair accessible

London Zoo was founded in 1826 and opened to the public two years later. Britain, then a major colonial power, was importing animals from around the globe. Visiting the zoo was most people's first sighting of such mythic beasts such as alligators, elephants, giraffes, kangaroos and pandas. Among the highlights are the penguin pool, the elephant and rhino pavilion and the aviary full of free-flying birds .

There are regular opportunities to 'meet the animals' and a new **Children's Zoo** where kids can stroke and pat friendly creatures and have their faces painted to look like a lizard or a tiger. Best of all is the *Web of Life* exhibition, which promotes conservation around the world. Housed in an eco-friendly glass building, it shows young visitors how different creatures have adapted to a variety of ecosystems. Visitors can learn more by playing on the computers and can have a go at brass rubbing or badge-making in the *Activity Den*.

Ozer

4–5 Langham Place, W1

Tel: (020) 7323 0505

Open: daily noon–2.30pm and 6–11pm.

Moderate

A plush interior to this restaurant, specializing in Turkish and North African food.

OXFORD CIRCUS

see **Victoria Line, p.164**
Oxford Street p.164, Regent Street p.165, Liberty p.165, Hamley's p.166, Carnaby Street p.167

PICCADILLY CIRCUS

see **Piccadilly Line, p.151**
Trocadero p.152, St James's Church,Piccadilly p.152

CHARING CROSS

see **Northern Line (Charing Cross branch), p.131**
Trafalgar Square p.131, St Martin-in-the-Fields p.132, National Gallery p.133, National Portrait Gallery p.135, Institute of Contemporary Arts p.136, Mall Galleries p.137

EMBANKMENT

see **Circle line, p.71**
Golden Jubilee Bridge p.71, Embankment Gardens p.71, Cleopatra's Needle p.72

Queen's Walk

WATERLOO

The Queen's Walk (5 mins)

This riverside walk runs along the South Bank from Westminster Bridge to Tower Bridge. You can walk in either direction from Waterloo – south along the Albert Embankment (with a view of the Houses of Parliament across the water), past the **London Eye** (*see* p.19) and **Saatchi Gallery** (*see* p.22) to the **Museum of Garden History** (*see* p.25) – or east towards London Bridge, taking in many of London's most popular attractions, such as the , the **South Bank Centre** (*see* p.23), the **Oxo Tower** (*see* p.99), **Tate Modern** (*see* p.97), **Shakespeare's Globe** (*see* p.105), **Vinopolis** (*see* p.105), **Borough Market** (*see* p.101), **HMS** *Belfast* (*see* p.120), **Tower Bridge** (*see* p.59), **Butlers Wharf** (*see* p.122) and the **Design Museum** (*see* p.123). Exploring the lot in one go will take you about four days; instead, be selective and enjoy the walk.

Cubana

48 Lower Marsh

Tel: (020) 7928 8778

Open: Mon–Sat 10am–midnight.

Moderate

With a large mural on its exterior wall, this is a great place for tapas and cocktails.

The London Eye (5 mins)

Tel: 0870 5000 600; www.ba-londoneye.com
Open: daily 9.30am–8pm; open until 9pm May and Sep Fri–Sun, Jun Mon–Thu; open until 10pm 22 May– 3 June daily, 3–30 Jun Fri–Sun, 1 July–5 Sep daily
Adm: adults £11.50, concessions £9.50, 5–15s £5.75, under-5s free but must be booked; 5% discount for online booking; advance and on-the-day tickets are available from the ticket office, but queues are long; 'flight time' is 30 mins; collect prebooked tickets 30 mins before. Combined flight ticket with river cruise available
Wheelchair accessible: two chairs per pod

The British Airways London Eye is everything the Millennium Dome at Greenwich should have been but wasn't: simple, cheap and popular. At 135m (440ft) with 32 capsules, each holding up to 25 people, the ride takes a gentle 30 minutes and affords 25-mile views. On a clear day you can see as far as Heathrow airport and Windsor Castle. Think twice if you are afraid of heights: the clear capsules and the panoramic views can be daunting and once you are in you can't get out. Also, when it is hot the capsules can get stuffy so take a drink. Hosted flights are available (call for details), giving you a guided tour of the view.

County Hall (7 mins)

County Hall Gallery
Tel: 0870 744 7485;
www.countyhallgallery.com
Open: daily 10am–6.30pm (last entry 5.30)
Adm: adults £9, concessions £7.50, 8–16s £5.50, 4–7s £3.50, families £24; further charge for special exhibitions
Wheelchair accessible

The splendidly sited County Hall, former home of the Greater London Council, is built on an ancient marsh where, during construction a Roman boat (now in the Museum of London, *see* p.46) was found. Architecturally, the building is loosely termed 'Edwardian Renaissance' and is

Thai Silk
103–107 Waterloo Road
Tel: (020) 7633 9886
Open: Mon–Sat noon–11pm
Moderate
Thai food is the speciality here, with excellent, friendly service and appropriate decor.

Waterloo Bar & Kitchen
131 Waterloo Rd
Tel: (020) 7928 5086
Open: Mon–Fri noon–2.45pm and 5.30–10.30pm
Moderate
Modern European food in an informal setting. Booking advised.

planned around several internal courtyards. The bright interior is marvellous, with marble foyers, oak panelling, carving and gilded ceilings – and a dash of municipal pride. It is home to several attractions, *see* below.

London Aquarium
Basement, County Hall
Tel: *(020) 7967 8000*
www.londonaquarium.co.uk
Open: *daily 10am–6pm, last entry 5pm*
Adm: *adults £9.75, concessions £7.50, 3–14s £6.25, families £29; Wheelchair accessible*

This is Europe's largest exhibition of global aquatic life, living in over two million litres of water. Arranged according to different water environments, it also gestures towards modern ecological concerns with an exhibit devoted to the declining rainforest and another to pollution in the River Thames. One of the biggest draws, apart from the sharks, is the touch pool where, if you manage to squeeze past the excitable toddlers, you can stroke some of the more benign fish, including a friendly giant ray.

Namco Station
County Hall, Riverside Building, Westminster Bridge Road, SE1
Tel: *(020) 7967 1066*
Open: *daily 10am–midnight*
Adm: *free (pay to play)*
Bar on the bottom floor
Two floors of shoot-'em-ups, space rides, driving simulators and pixelated kick-boxers. This is heaven for game players of all ages. If you are not used to it, the bright lights and frenzied bashing of buttons and tugging of levers can get a bit much and the machines guzzle pound coins with glee. But

The London Aquarium

if you like simulators, arcade games, bumper cars, American pool, ten-pin bowling or shooting ranges, Namco Station is fun – as long as your wallet holds out.

Saatchi Gallery
County Hall, Riverside Building,
Westminster Bridge Road, SE1
***Tel**: (020) 7823 2363 or 7928 8195*
www.saatchi-gallery.co.uk
***Open**: Sun–Thu 10am–8pm, Fri–Sat 10am–10pm*
***Adm**: adults £8.75, concessions £6.75,*
prebooked tickets £5.25, family £26.

Saatchi, a modern-day Medici, is famous for his patronage of Young British Artists, a movement whose original exponents are Damien Hirst, Sarah Lucas and Gary Hume, but now includes Tracey Emin, Gavin Turk, Jenny Saville, Marc Quinn and Jake and Dinos Chapman, among others. The collection (which moved from a white space in St John's Wood in 2003) sits incongruously in its surroundings, although apparently, this is part of Saatchi's intention – to challenge what is now the conventional method of exhibiting modern art.

On entering one feels compelled to pass quickly through the few rooms of recent acquisitions in order to find *The Shark* and *My Bed*.... Emin's bed is rather disappointing, sitting rather pathetically amid its litter of condoms, tissues and cigarette butts; Hirst's series of eerie pickled mammals, here represented by *The Physical Impossibility of Death in the Mind of Someone Living and Away from the Flock*, were the first pieces of BritArt to capture the public's attention and/or imagination. Other interesting pieces include, Ron Mueck's *Angel* and *Dead Dad*, Turner Prize-winner (2003) Grayson Perry's brilliant but unhappy vases, Gavin Turk's *Nomad*, Marc Quinn's *Self* (a head made of frozen blood) and Belinda de Bruyckere's awkwardly posed and slightly disturbing *(Horse) K27*. The power of these pieces, like many in the gallery, lies in the confrontation between viewer and subject.

Dalí Universe Exhibition
Tel: *0870 744 7485;*
www.countyhallgallery.com
Open: *daily 10am–6.30pm (last entry 5.30)*
Adm: *adults £9, concessions £7.50, 8–16s £5.50,*
4–7s £3.50, families £24; further charge for
special exhibitions
Wheelchair accessible

The permanent Dalí Universe exhibition shows
a retrospective of Surrealist Spanish artist
Salvador Dalí and contains many of his famous
pieces, including his sofa created in the shape
of Mae West's lips. It has the largest collection
of Dalí sculptures, including melting clocks and
double-jointed elephants carrying pyramids.
There is also work by Marc Chagall and
Picasso, as well as temporary exhibits.

IMAX Cinema (5 mins)
1 Charlie Chaplin Walk, Waterloo SE1 (exit 5,
follow the signposted pedestrian subways)
Tel: *0870 787 252;*
www.bfi.org.uk/showing/imax/
Wheelchair accessible

At over 20m high, this is the UK's biggest
cinema screen. Daily screenings of 3-D and
occasional new, large-format 2-D movies,
such as *Batman Begins*.

South Bank Centre (8 mins)
South Bank, SE1
Tel: *(020) 7928 6143; www.sbc.org.uk*

This riverside arts complex is currently
undergoing a facelift but is still an
invigorating place to go, day or night. If you
are not attending an event, you can sit
outside the NFT and sip a cool beer, sift
through the second-hand books and prints

on sale under the bridge, stroll along the river towards **Gabriel's Wharf** (*see* p.99), where you may see a fire-eater or juggling comedian, or watch skateboarders as they hop about trying out new tricks.

Royal Festival Hall, Queen Elizabeth Hall and Purcell Room (5 mins)
South Bank, SE1
Tel: *(020) 7921 0600; www.rfh.org.uk*

Large and airy, with a good bar, bookshop and café, this is one of the top venues in the country for classical music. It also hosts occasional free exhibitions.

Hayward Gallery (8 mins)
Belvedere Road, South Bank Centre, SE1
Tel: *(020) 7960 4242 www.hayward.org.uk*
Open: *10am–6 daily, until 8 on Wed and Thur*
Adm: *varies (phone for details)*

Scrunched behind the Festival Hall like an aged spaceship (but marvellous inside),the Hayward is an art exhibition space and puts on diverse shows throughout the year.

National Film Theatre (9 mins)
South Bank, SE1
Tel: *(020) 7928 3232;*
www.bfi.org.uk/showing/nft

The NFT does a good line in classic screenings, previews and special intervies. there is a children's matinée at the weekend.

Royal National Theatre (10 mins)
South Bank, SE1
Tel: *(020) 7452 3400;*
www.nationaltheatre.org.uk
Open: *(box office) 10am–8 daily*
Tours: Mon-Sat, three times a day (adm: adults £5, concessions £4). Book in advance or ask at the information desk in the main foyer

The Royal National Theatre is actually three theatres (the Olivier, Lyttleton and the Cottesloe) and caters for everything from large-scale razzmatazz to contemporary drama and razor-edged fringe. If you don't see a performace (and even if you do) take the opportunity to follow a fascinating behind-the-scenes tour.

Mezzanine Royal National Theatre
Tel: (020) 7452 3600
Open: Mon–Sat noon–11pm
Moderate
Modern Eurpean cuisine with fast, efficient waiter service.

Terrace Café Royal National Theatre
Tel: (020) 7452 3600
Open: Mon–Sat noon–11pm
Moderate
Fresh, grill-style food (including vegetarian options), overlooking the Thames.

The Royal National Theatre

Florence Nightingale Museum (8 mins)

St Thomas's Hospital, Lambeth Palace Road SE1
Tel: *(020) 7620 0374*
www.florence-nightingale.co.uk
Open: *Mon–Fri 10am–5pm, Sat, Sun and bank hol Mon 10am–4.30pm, last adm 1 hr before closing*
Adm: *adults £5.80, concessions and children £4.20, families £13*
Shop; Wheelchair accessible

Housed in St Thomas's Hospital, where Florence Nightingale founded the world's first school of nursing over 100 years ago, this museum (entrance on the right as you go in) presents the indomitable woman at various stages in her life through personal artefacts, paintings, set-pieces, quotations and storyboards. There are also letters and school books from her privileged schooldays and a medicine chest she took to the Crimea.

Courtyard Café Museum of Garden History

Tel: (020) 7401 8865
Open: Daily
10.30am–4.30pm
Moderate
Home-made hot food, including vegetarian options and cakes.

Museum of Garden History (10 mins)

Parish Church of St Mary-at-Lambeth, Lambeth Palace Road, SE1
Tel: *(020) 7401 8865;*
www.museumgardenhistory.org
Open: *Mar–mid Dec daily 10.30am–5pm*
Adm: *donation of £3 (concessions £2.50)*
Café; Wheelchair accessible

This delightful museum is housed in Lambeth's old parish church (the tower is 14th-century) in whose graveyard are buried the Tradescants, father and son, 16th–17th-century gardeners and plant importers, who were responsible for the introduction of many (for the time) new and exotic plants, such as pomegranates, orange trees, figs and peaches.

They are also credited with introducing the pineapple to Britain as an ornamental motif – you can see examples of this on Lambeth Bridge – and are commemorated in one of the museum windows.

Museum of Garden History

Part of the museum exhibits garden tools dating from the mid-19th century on, others are organized in a social context, exploring the links between types of home and garden: hence the Country House, the Suburban House and the Urban Experience. Another section focuses on intrepid British plant hunters and vegetal curiosities.

There is a pretty knot garden in the graveyard, and nearby you can find the grave of Captain Bligh of the HMS *Bounty*.

Imperial War Museum (5 mins)

Lambeth Road SE1; turn left on Westminster Bridge Road
Tel: *(020) 7416 5320; www.iwm.org.uk*
Open: *daily 10am–6pm*
Adm: *free, charge for special exhibitions*
Children's activities, shop, café
Mostly wheelchair accessible

Considering some people's belief that war is insanity, it is appropriate that the museum is housed in the former Bethlehem Royal Hospital, otherwise known as Bedlam, where the sad and deranged were kept during the 17th and 18th centuries to the amusement of the public who came to snigger at the lunatics. It now houses one of the capital's best attractions with an incomparable collection of war memorabilia.

The first sight you see is the massive 37cm (15 in) naval guns, weighing 100 tons each, which could propel a 1,925lb shell 29km (18 miles). Inside the atrium, there are other large exhibits such as a restored Jagdpanther tank destroyer, a Supermarine Spitfire and a V2 rocket. Children love it all and happily step into the bowels of a cramped Halifax

Imperial War Museum Café
Tel: (020) 7416 5439
Open: Daily 10.30am - 5.30pm
Inexpensive
Offer a wide selection of fresh dishes, prepared on the premises. The Café is licensed and there is also a wholesome children's menu.

bomber or take on the role of a pilot in a flight simulator (extra payment required).

The basement is devoted to the two World Wars. As you enter, you see a clock counting the number of people killed in war, a number that goes up by two per minute. As well as the huge collection of uniforms, weaponry, equipment and memorabilia there are two 'experiences'. The *Trench Experience* lets you grope your way through a dingy (and smelly) trench during World War I. In the *Blitz Experience* you are in a London street as fires rage and doodlebugs pound the city. *Secret War* on the first floor looks at the world of espionage and has lots of buttons to press (can you crack the 'Enigma' code?). On the second floor is the museum art collection, including work by Henry Moore, John Singer Sargent and Stanley Spencer.

The most moving exhibit is in the newer top two floors. *The Holocaust Exhibition* charts the rise of Hitler and the Nazi party to the horror of the Final Solution and its aftermath. An accompanying exhibition explores the theme of genocide in *Crimes Against Humanity*. After this you may want to step outside where there is a Tibetan Peace Garden, opened by His Holiness The Dalai Lama in 1999.

The Imperial War Museum

St Paul's Cathedral

CENTRAL LINE

'Yesterday the crowds swayed and surged to get on to the trains. It was a cosmopolitan throng. Nearly every civilized nation under the sun was represented among the humanity that was struggling to experience London's latest sensation.' So ran the Daily Mail, reporting on the opening of the Central Line in 1900. The new line was a success from the start, carrying 84,500 passengers on its first day. It soon became known as the 'Twopenny Tube' because of its affordable fare of 2d (just under one new penny) for a ride from Shepherd's Bush to Bank. The carriages were of a new design and pulled by rather heavy electric motors, which caused some residents living above ground to complain that their houses shook when the trains passed underneath.

HOLLAND PARK

Holland Park (3 mins)

Holland Park Avenue; cross the road from the station and turn left, then take the first right into Holland Park road; the entrance is 300m along on the left-hand side
Tel: *(020) 7471 9813;*
www.friendsofhollandpark.org.uk
Open: *summer 8am–8pm, winter 8am–4.30pm*
Adm: *free*
Opera Holland Park: **Tel**: *0845 230 9769, www.operahollandpark.com;* **Ice House art gallery**: *open daily 11am–7pm, adm free, tel: (020) 7602 3316*

This piece of countryside in West London is part of the old estate of Holland House, a Jacobean mansion that was built around 1606 for Sir Walter Cope, who was Chancellor of the Exchequer for James I. The lower storey of the main house, its East Wing, Ice House and Orangery are all that remain after World War II bombing and subsequent years of dereliction.

The landscaped surroundings are a blissful place to be at any time of the year, with formal gardens and woodland to explore (ubiquitous squirrels aplenty), and dotted with sculpture and ornamental fountains. The *East Wing* is home to a youth hostel; the lower storey of the main house serves as a backdrop for theatre and acclaimed opera in summer (**see** above for contact details); the small *Ice House* is now a modern venue for art exhibitions (**see** above for contact details); and the pleasingly light-filled, larger *Orangery Gallery* is another popular contemporary art space. In addition, there is a children's playground, a wildlife pond, sports and games facilities and an ecology visitor centre.

NOTTING HILL GATE

see Circle Line, p.52

Portobello Market p.52

Julie's Wine Bar

135–137 Portland Rd, W11

Tel: (020) 7221 1992

Open: for food Mon–Sat 12.30–2.45pm and 7.30–11pm, Sun 12.30–3.30pm and 7.30–10pm; afternoon tea served daily 3–7.30pm

Inexpensive

Café-cum-wine-bar-cum restaurant, with slightly overdone decor. Best for afternoon tea.

Books for Cooks

4 Blenheim Crescent, W11

Tel: (020) 7221 1992

Open: Mon–Sat 9.30am–6pm

Inexpensive

A bit of an oddity. A book shop with a restaurant where you can try out some of the recipes from the volumes on sale.

Marble Arch, Park Lane

MARBLE ARCH

Marble Arch (2 mins)
Corner of Park Lane and Marble Arch Road

This white triumphal gateway is the work
of John Nash, that architectural *maestro* of
the Regency period (1811-20). It wasn't
actually intended for this spot, but was
Nash's gateway to his 1827 creation,
Buckingham Palace (*see* p.74). Nash ran to
such extravagance with the project – a
third over-budget – that eventually he was
dismissed from the job. The fate of the
Arch was determined in 1847 by a lack of
bedroom space in the Palace for Queen
Victoria and Prince Albert; in order to make
room for the construction of the East Front
(the side you see now from the Mall) the
Marble Arch was removed and later
reconstructed on its present site.

The island Marble Arch sits on is also the
site of the old Tyburn gallows, London's
main place of execution from 1388 to 1783,
where over 500,000 people met their end.
Among these were Perkin Warbeck, a
pretender to the throne (1499),
Archbishop Oliver Plunkett who was
beheaded by Cromwell's troops (1681),
and Oliver Cromwell himself, whose body
was exhumed from Westminster Abbey
(*see* p.92) after the Restoration in 1660,
gibbeted, beheaded and, it is said, buried
in a pit nearby.

Hyde Park (3 mins)

Tel: *(020) 7298 2100; www.royalparks.gov.uk*
Open: *daily 5am–midnight*; *Adm*: *free*

Hyde Park is London's lung, a calm, green breathing space in the centre of the city, that merges in the west with Kensington Gardens (*see* p.82). The boundary between them roughly runs from the Victoria Gate in the north to the Alexandra Gate in the south.

The park, once Henry VIII's private hunting ground, was not open to the public until the 17th century, when May Day tours around the Ring became fashionable, and coach races were also popular. (In one race Oliver Cromwell whipped his horses so much that he was flung from his coach, caught his foot in the tackle, and was dragged along the ground while his pistol went off in his pocket.) London's first-ever street lighting was installed here when William III had 300 lamps hung along the *route de roi* (from which the name 'Rotten Row' derives) to deter robbers and highwaymen. In the 18th century disputes were settled here by duel, and in 1730 the L-shaped Serpentine lake was created by Queen Caroline when she had the Westbourne River dammed.

The *Princess Diana Memorial Fountain*, opened in 2004, is close to the Serpentine bridge and was sculpted to reflect the changes in her life. You can also go boating on the Serpentine, swim at the *Lido* (open end Jun–8 Sep), play tennis, skateboard or rollerblade, cycle along special cycle paths, ride horses at the *manège*, or snooze away the afternoon in a striped deckchair (Apr–Sep) and, unlike some other parks, play about on the grass as much as you like. There are three good cafés and several refreshment points selling ice cream. The squirrels are tame and partial to chocolate, which probably accounts for their size.

Speakers' Corner (4 mins)

Northeast corner of Hyde Park

People have been letting off steam at Speakers' Corner since 1872, when the government recognized the right of

Hyde Park Rose Garden

assembly here. The name indicates a freedom of speech and, indeed, anyone who has a mind may speak here on any subject, be it Jesus Christ, Karl Marx or the medicinal benefits of bananas – provided they are not blasphemous or obscene, and do not incite a breach of the peace (although today it is unlikely the former two would be policed). The right was exercised most memorably in 2003, when a large demonstration against the war in Iraq culminated in Hyde Park, despite government attempts to prevent it from happening – one claim was that protestors would damage the grass.

Sofra

1 St Christopher's Place, W1

Tel: (020) 7224 4080

Open: noon–11.45pm daily

Inexpensive

Authentic Turkish restaurant tucked away in a little square. Friendly staff. Terrace in fine weather.

BOND STREET

Sir Thomas Bond was the principal speculator in this area in the 1680s, and his name was given to what is now one of the world's most exclusive shopping streets. Built in two stages, the original 'Old' Bond Street lies at the southern end of this road, the only one to link Oxford Street and Piccadilly (*see* p.164 and 151); the northern stretch, New Bond Street, dates from the early 1720s. Here, and in the streets running off it, you will find exclusive boutiques for clothes (Chanel, Ralph Lauren, Dolce & Gabbana, Gucci, Prada, Versace, Hardy Amies, Miu Miu, Yves Saint Laurent, Prada), shoes and accessories (Jimmy Choo, Louis Vuitton, Sergio Rossi) and jewellery (Asprey, Cartier, De Beers, Garrard, Swarovski, Tiffany); there is also the super-priced department store, Fenwick.

If your wallet is less than overburdened, there are more modestly priced shops nearby: **South Molton Street** is shoe shop heaven and, of course, there is **Oxford Street**, with Selfridges (*see* below), Debenhams, House of Fraser and John Lewis, and many more familiar chains.

Handel House Museum (3 mins)

25 Brook Street, W1 (south of Bond St station, entrance at the rear, on Lancashire Court)
***Tel**: (020) 7495 1685; www.handelhouse.org*
***Open**: Tue–Sat 10am–6pm, Thu until 8pm, Sun and hols noon–6pm*
***Adm**: adults £4.50, concessions £3.50, children £2 (free on Sat afternoons, with drop-in activities)*
Gift shop; Wheelchair accessible; ring in advance

George Frideric Handel spent a total of 50 years in London and for his last 36, he lived here in Brook Street, from 1723 to 1759. He came to London originally because of the popularity of Italian opera here, but his appointment as composer to the Royal Chapel at St James's Palace in 1723 must also have influenced his move. Handel composed some of his most famous works in this house, among them *Zadok the Priest*, the *Music for the Royal Fireworks* and *The Messiah*, which he wrote in three weeks.

Despite the removal in 1905 of the entire façade and interior panelling up to the second floor, the museum – with creaking, higgledy-piggledy floors and walls – manages to re-create an essence of the early 18th century and Handel's life in London surprisingly effectively, particularly if you're lucky and a visiting musician is trying out an instrument. Items on view include portraits of Handel's musicians and singers, two reproduction harpsichords, the famous portrait of Handel by Philip Mercier and one of the wealthy and, by all accounts, pompous Charles Jennens, librettist of *The Messiah*. There's also a handwritten score of Mozart's arrangement of a Handel string quartet; several first editions of printed scores; and, odd but interesting, a small exhibition of photos of Jimi Hendrix, who lived in the house next door between 1968 and 1969.

Selfridges

400 Oxford Street, W1

Tel: 0870 837 7377; www.selfridges.co.uk

Open: Mon–Fri 10am–8pm, Sat 9.30am–8pm, Sun noon–6pm

Inexpensive

Selfridges's 20 eateries include the Moët champagne bar, the Food Garden Café (Lebanese, Indian and SE Asian), Iguazu (Latin American), the Oyster Bar, Brass Rail (North American diner), Café 400 (pizza), Momo (North African) and Seaty Pretzels (a juice and salad bar), as well as Eat, Espresso and Haagen Dazs cafés, a Starbucks and a Yo Sushi restaurant.

Selfridges (3 mins)

400 Oxford Street, W1
***Tel**: 0870 837 7377; www.selfridges.co.uk*
***Open**: Mon–Fri 10am–8pm, Sat 9.30am–8pm, Sun noon–6pm*
Wheelchair accessible

North of the station, this bastion of London shopping, opened in 1909, was founded by one Harry Gordon Selfridge, of Wisconsin, USA. He introduced new ideas to London retail with the open-plan layout of his store and having goods on display and accessible rather than behind counters. he is also credited with coining the phrase, 'The customer is always right'.

Much of the interior was completed in the 1920s in Art Deco style. Once you have entered this enormous store, you may need

The Queen of Time, the Art-Deco bronze statue over the entrance of Selfridges

a compass to find your way out; but this is the place to find anything and everything, be it stationery, pens, handbags, cosmetics, clothes or chocolate. Selfridges still has one of the best food halls in town, but if you want a drink or a bite to eat on the spot, there are 20 places to try here.

The Wallace Collection (10 mins)

Hertford House, Manchester Square, W1
Tel: *(020) 7593 9500*
www.wallacecollection.org
Open: *Mon–Sat 10am–5pm, Sun noon–5pm;*
Adm: *by donation; charge for special exhibitions*
Free guided tours: *Mon–Fri 1pm, Wed and Sat 11.30am, Sun 3pm (but sometimes replaced by specialist talks; call or see website for details)*
Audioguide available; gift shop and café
Wheelchair accessible

Assembled by four successive Marquesses of Hertford and the 4th Marquess's illegitimate son, Sir Richard Wallace, this collection occupies 25 galleries in the former family home. A 10-minute walk north of Bond Street, you will rarely find throngs of visitors, which makes it all the more pleasant to saunter round this stunning 18th-century mansion house. Many of the 5,470 items on display are paintings, including Frans Hals' *Laughing Cavalier* and masterpieces by Canaletto, Rubens, Rembrandt and Velasquez. It also has an excellent French 18th-century collection, to rival that in the Louvre, featuring works by Boucher, Watteau and Fragonard. Besides these, there are some choice pieces of furniture, Sèvres porcelain and, on the ground floor, a huge collection of armour, including a terrifying war harness for man and horse from South Germany *c.* 1475–85.

Despite the formal setting, the Wallace Collection is child-friendly. A year-round Wheely Cart offers the wherewithal for various activities and the Collection organizes imaginative workshops for kids during the holidays, such as designing dolls' dresses, armour handling and art classes with established artists (phone ahead for details). A refit by architect Rick

---

Café Bagatelle

The Wallace Collection

Tel: (020) 7563 9505

Open: Mon–Sat 10am–4.30pm.

Moderate

Good food in a fantastic airy 'outdoor' setting surrounded by the museum's fabulous collection.

No.6 George Street

6 George St, W1

Tel: (020) 7935 1910

Open: Mon–Fri 8am–5.30pm.

Moderate

Deli and small dining room serving high quality fresh food, such as wild salmon fishcakes, leek and cheddar soufflé and stem-ginger ice cream.

De Gustibus

53 Blandford St, W1

Tel: (020) 7486 6608; www.degustibus.co.uk

Open: Mon–Fri 7am–4.30pm, Sat 9am–3pm

Inexpensive

Traditional bakery. Good for coffee, cakes and snacks

Union Café

96 Marylebone Lane

Tel: (020) 7486 4860

Open: Mon–Sat 12.30–3pm and 6.30–10.30pm

Inexpensive

Good-value, simple, modern European food, using organic produce in an informal setting.

The Wallace Collection, Manchester Square

Mather in 2000 added four new galleries and a study centre, plus an all-weather sculpture garden and café.

OXFORD CIRCUS

see **Victoria line, p.164**

Oxford Street p.164, Regent Street p.165, Liberty p.165, Hamley's p.166, Carnaby Street p.167

TOTTENHAM COURT ROAD

British Museum (10 mins)

Great Russell Street, WC1
Tel: (020) 7323 8299
www.thebritishmuseum.ac.uk
Open: Sat–Wed 10am–5.30pm, Thu–Fri 10am–8.30pm
Adm: by donation (adm for temporary exhibitions is usually about £7 for adults, £3.50 for concessions)
Audio tours, guided tours and talks; ask for details at the information desks
Two cafés and a restaurant
Wheelchair accessible (see website)

The British Museum is the country's most visited tourist attraction, a treasure house with 100 galleries, and some of mankind's greatest relics. You'd need a week to fully appreciate the sheer volume of objects here, which range from Greek and Roman artefacts, Tibetan painting and African textiles to medieval headgear, Venetian

glass and Japanese prints, with a lot more besides. Just head directly to what you think is most interesting – though you are bound to be waylaid *en route*.

By far the most popular exhibits, especially among children, are the dead people. The *Ancient Egyptian Galleries* (Rooms 62–66) have mummies galore as well as a menagerie of their companions including mummified cats, fish and livestock. *Lindow Man* in Room 50 also has a strange fascination. This leathery looking Briton was ritually slain, perhaps as a sacrifice, in the 1st century AD and lay perfectly preserved in a Cheshire peat marsh until he was uncovered by archaeologists in 1984.

Also not to be missed are the *Elgin Marbles* (Room 8), the frieze reliefs from the Parthenon in Athens which, depending on whom you believe, were either rescued or stolen by Lord Elgin, British Ambassador to the Ottoman Empire, in 1802. Carved in about 440 BC to decorate Athena's temple on the Acropolis, they depict a festival to commemorate Athena's birthday, which includes a grand procession of chariots, musicians, pitcher bearers, sacrificial victims and beautiful women as well as the gods Hermes and Dionysus.

The British Museum's other famous exhibits include the *Rosetta Stone* (Room 25), inscribed with the same decree in three languages, which allowed Egyptian hieroglyphics to be deciphered for the first time, and the *Sutton Hoo Treasure* (Room 41), a jewel-encrusted collection of swords,

Court Restaurant
British Museum
Tel: (020) 7323 8990
Open: Sat-Wed 11am – 12pm coffee only, 12pm-3pm Lunch 3pm-5pm tea; Thu–Fri also 5.30pm-9pm dinner
Moderate
Mostly Mediterranean – inspired fare. Overlooking the reading room and up close to the fantastic glass roof

Abeno Okonomi-yaki
47 Museum Street
Tel: (020) 7405 3211
Moderate
Japanese restaurant specializing in okonomi-yaki (like a tortilla), which are theatrically cooked at your table.

Townhouse Brasserie
24 Coptic Street, WC1
Tel: (020) 7636 2731
Open: Mon–Fri 8.30am–3pm and 6–11pm, Sat–Sun 9am–3pm and 6–11pm
Expensive
Sophisticated French eatery, with a special children's eating area in the basement.

Savoir Faire

42 New Oxford Street, WC1

Tel: (020) 7436 0707

Inexpensive

A small French eaterie serving bistro food at rock-bottom prices.

The Lamb

Lamb's Conduit Street, WC1

Tel: (020) 7405 0713

Open: Mon–Sat 11am–11pm, Sun noon–4pm, 7–10.30pm

Inexpensive

A little way from both the British Museum and Sir John Soane's Museum, but worth the walk for the fine beers and the ornate, hinged glass panels that separate the staff from the public.

Princess Louise

208 High Holborn, WC1

Tel: (020) 7405 8816

Open: Mon–Fri 11am–11pm, Sat noon–11pm

Inexpensive

Huge Victorian pub magnificently decorated with ornate crimson- and gold-moulded ceilings, etched gilt mirrors and fruit-shaped tiles. It's a listed building, and even the gents' has a preservation order. Best for drinks rather than food.

helmets, bowls and buckles from Europe.

After the British Library (*see* p. 163) was moved to Euston, the museum underwent a massive overhaul with the construction of a glass ceiling over the Greek Revival courtyard at the centre of the building. The spectacular domed reading room at the centre of this **Great Court** is now open to the public for the first time in 150 years. The massive King's Library, built between 1823 and 1827 to house the library of George III, was long used for storing some of the British Library's collection; this was also opened up and now houses a permanent exhibition on learning and discovery in 18th-century Britain.

HOLBORN

Sir John Soane's Museum (3 mins)

13 Lincoln's Inn Fields, WC2
Tel: *(020) 7405 2107; www.soane.org*
Open: *Tue–Sat 10am–5pm*
Adm: *by donation*
Guided tour: *Sat at 2.30pm (£3); visits by candlelight on the first Tue of each month 6–9pm*
Ground floor wheelchair accessible, though narrow in places

Sir John Soane (1753–1837), son of a bricklayer and architect of the Bank of England (*see* p.114), was one of this country's great eccentrics as well as being one of the finest architects of his age. In his later years, he bought three houses on Lincoln's Inn Fields and transformed them into an extraordinary treasure trove, full of nooks and crannies, for his huge collection of paintings, sculpture and curiosities, including Christopher Wren's watch and a monument to his wife's dog. Among the highlights are Hogarth's *Rake's Progress* in the picture room (also famous for Soane's ingenious hinged walls) and the sarcophagus of the Egyptian Pharaoh Seti I, but it is the house itself that is the star of the show. Odd angles, sudden drops, mysterious little rooms, domed skylights,

The Sir John Soane's Museum, Lincoln's Inn Fields

and craftily placed mirrors and windows make exploring this museum a delightful experience.

CHANCERY LANE

At Chancery Lane you enter legal London, home to the Inns of Court. The area's association with law goes back to the 14th century, when Edward III moved the Keeper of the Rolls of Chancery here and the old Inns of Chancery were established; the buildings of one of them, **Staple Inn**, stand on the south side of High Holborn, behind a 16th-century timber-frame façade that was originally a wool warehouse (hence the 'staple'). Members of this Inn obviously had their cranky days, evident from a sign that hangs in the entrance passage, telling street vendors and 'rude' children to be quiet.

You can explore the buildings, lanes and alleyways of the **Inns of Court** from here. Some buildings date from as far back as the 12th century; be aware that, apart from the churches, you can't actually go inside – unless you're good at charming security guards. These 'honorable societies' provide support for barristers and students, and one of their their key purposes, for which they alone hold responsibility and power, is

Konditor & Cook

46 Gray's Inn Road, WC1

Tel: (020) 7404 6300

Inexpensive

Fabulous bakery and patisserie, which also serves hot and cold food, such as bacon and gruyère tartlets, pizza slices, salads, sandwiches, cakes and pastries.

Lincoln's Inn

to call barristers to the Bar. There are four Inns today: Gray's Inn, Middle and Inner Temple (*see* p.65), and **Lincoln's Inn**. The latter is the nearest, with its medieval *Old Hall* (1492; ask permission to see inside); Tudor gatehouse on Chancery Lane (look for the statues of Thomas More and Thomas Lovell, who were both members of the Inn); early 17th-century chapel with a fan-vaulted undercroft; Palladian stone buildings and late 17th-century *New Square*. What with the Inns' traditions, black-clad barristers striding the cobbles and porters scurrying about, their trolleys laden with legal documents, you will encounter more than a whiff of the past here.

On Chancery Lane itself you will also see the splendid neo-Gothic building of the former **Public Records Office** (1831), now the Maughan Library of King's College.

St Etheldreda's Church (5 mins)

14 Ely Place, Holborn Circus, EC1N
***Tel**: (020) 7405 1061*
***Open**: Mon–Fri 7am–7pm*
***Adm**: by donation*

At the east end of High Holborn, this church, the last surviving part of the medieval palace of the Bishops of Ely, dates from *c*.1293. It is dedicated to St Etheldreda, a 7th-century East Anglian princess who founded and became abbess of a double monastery, and was famous for her holiness and spiritual guidance. It is built in two tiers: an upper church for the bishop to pray in and a crypt for the locals. It is the oldest surviving Catholic church in London and the palace, of which it was part, is mentioned in Shakespeare's plays *Richard II* and *Richard III*.

The wonderfully atmospheric crypt dates from around 1251, but incorporates earlier walls. A model shows how large the palace would have been. In the upper church you are nearly bowled over by the brilliance of the east window, created by Edward Nuttgens and completed in 1952 (this part of the chapel suffered damage during World War II and all of the glass is post-war). The screen is late

Ye Old Mitre Tavern
Ely Court, EC1N (through alleyway between Ely Place and Hatton Garden)

Tel: (020) 7405 4751

Inexpensive

This cosy, wood-panelled pub's name reflects the local historical connection with the Ely bishops and, indeed, it is an 18th-century replacement for an earlier tavern built for the bishops' servants. Serves real ales and bar snacks.

Victorian and by Francis Bentley, architect of Westminster Cathedral (*see* p.173). The figures on the walls represent local Catholic martyrs who would have known the chapel.

In 1874 St Etheldreda's was the first-ever pre-Reformation site of worship to be restored to the Roman Catholic Church.

Prince Henry's Room, *see* p.70

Dr Johnson's House (10 mins)
17 Gough Square (off Fleet Street), EC4
Tel: *(020) 7353 3745; www.drjh.dircon.co.uk*
Open: *May–Sept Mon–Sat 11am–5.30pm; Oct–Apr Mon–Sat 11am–5pm*
Adm: *adult £4, concessions £4, children £1 (under-10s free)*
Gift shop

South of Chancery Lane, this 17th-century house was home to Doctor Samuel Johnson, lexicographer, author, critic and wit, from 1748 to 1759. His *Dictionary* of 1755, still interesting for the vigour and humour of its definitions (lexicographer = a writer of dictionaries, a harmless drudge), was mostly written here in the attic room where the good Doctor perched on a three-legged stool and barked orders at his six

The Café at the Crypt
St Etheldreda's Church

Tel: (020) 7242 8238

Open: Mon–Fri 12am–2pm, Sat noon–11pm

Inexpensive

Delicious hot and cold dishes in the pretty cloister. All main dishes under a fiver.

Bleeding Heart Tavern
Bleeding Heart Yard 19 Grenville St, EC1

Tel: (020) 7404 0333

Open: Mon–Fri 7am-12 midnight

Moderate

Cheaper French fare from the Bleeding Heart stable . Lovely food and lovely French waiters! Take your time and enjoy!

Dr Johnson's House, Gough Square

clerks. Not much in the house actually belonged to Johnson but the re-created rooms manage to convey a good impression of what life was like at a time when literary London was coming of age and Johnson and his pals (including such luminaries as Joshua Reynolds, Oliver Goldsmith, David Garrick and Edmund Burke) caroused till morning discussing philosophy, art, religion, politics and the relative merits of London's brothels

Temple Church, *see* p.70

ST PAUL'S ⭘

Temple Bar (1 min)

To the north of the main entrance of St Paul's Cathedral (*see* below) is Christopher Wren's Temple Bar gateway, which, after 30 years of planning, was returned to the City of London in 2004, having stood in exile on an estate in Hertfordshire since 1888. It was one of several that once marked the City's boundaries and originally stood on Fleet Street, at the western edge of the City where it was also used to display the heads of people who had been executed. It was removed in 1878 because of the construction

Temple Bar

of the Royal Courts of Justice and to ease traffic. The original royal statues (of Charles I, Charles II, James I and Anne of Denmark) have been restored and there are new statues of royal beasts and coats of arms. Just behind, in the newly developed Paternoster Square is the **Paternoster Column**; 18m (60ft) high and surmounted by a golden flaming torch, it replicates the Corinthian columns of the portico entrance to old St Paul's Cathedral, which burned in the Great Fire of 1666.

St Paul's Cathedral (3 mins)

St Paul's Churchyard, EC4
Tel: 020 7236 6883;
www.stpaulscathedral.org.uk
Open: Mon–Sat 8.30am–4pm
Adm: adults £7, concessions £6, children £3, family £17; Guided tours at 11am, 11.30am, 1.30pm, 2pm (adults £2.50, concessions £2, children £1); audioguide £3.50
Café and restaurant; gift shop
Wheelchair accessible via entrance on south side, but no wheelchair access to galleries

St Paul's Cathedral, the masterpiece of Sir Christopher Wren, was completed in 1710, 44 years after the Great Fire destroyed the old Cathedral. Wren had already been commissioned to repair the Norman building when it burnt down. Besides the sheer scale of the project, his chief headache was getting his ideas approved. His first plan (known as the New Model) never made it past the drawing board; his second (the Great Model), also rejected, is displayed in the crypt. It was only when Wren agreed to have a spire rather than an expensive dome that his third plan, known as the Warrant Design, was finally accepted. Fortunately, it was agreed that he could 'make some variations rather ornamental than essential, as from time to time he should see proper'. In the end, Wren changed quite a lot and reverted to many of his original ideas – including putting the dome back on top.

It is worth the entry price just to stand

Crypt Café
St Paul's Cathedral
Tel: (020) 7236 4128
Open Mon-Sat 9am-5pm; Sun 10am-5pm
Inexpensive
Light snacks, salads and homemade cakes, beer and wine after 11am.

Refectory Restaurant
St Paul's Cathedral
Tel: (020) 7236 4128
Open: Mon–Sun 11.30am - 5pm
Moderate
Serves lunch and tea – on Sunday come for the roast

St Paul's Cathedral, St Paul's Courtyard

The Black Friar

174 Queen Victoria Street, EC4

Tel: (020) 7236 5474

Open: Mon–Fri 11am–11pm

Inexpensive

Pub with Arts and Crafts interior with mother of pearl, wood carvings, stained glass and marble pillars.

under the dazzlingly ornate dome and look up. From here you can make you way up the 627 steps past the *Whispering Gallery* (where, if it is quiet enough, you can hear someone whisper 107 feet away), the *Stone Gallery* (encircling the outside of the dome) and the *Outer Golden Gallery* (providing one of the best views to be had in the city). Look west for the British Telecom Tower (formally the Post Office Tower), northwest for the Old Bailey (*see* p.46), south for Tate Modern (*see* p.97) , east for Canary Wharf and towards the river for Tower Bridge (*see* p.59).

There are also several important memorials, including, in the south choir aisle, one to the poet John Donne, who was Dean of the old St Paul's for ten years and a memorial to Wren, directly under the dome, which bears the inscription (in Latin): 'Reader, if you seek his monument, look around you.' In the crypt, a black sarcophagus (made from the mast of a vanquished French flagship) contains the remains of the British naval hero Admiral Nelson who died at the Battle of Trafalgar in 1805 and was pickled in alcohol before his final journey home.

From here, it's a short walk across the Millenium bridge (*see* p.98) to Tate Modern and the rest of the South Bank.

The Old Bailey (the Central Criminal Court) (5 mins)

Corner of Newgate Street and Old Bailey, EC4
***Tel**: (020) 7248 3277*
***Open**: Mon–Fri 10am–1pm and 2–5pm; closed bank hols and the following day*
***Adm**: free; Guided tours: Tue, Fri, Sat 11am, 2pm*
***Note**: strictly no cameras, large bags, drink, food, mobile phones, pagers, radios, gas canisters, etc allowed; no children under 14*
Wheelchair accessible

The Old Bailey

There has been a court on this site, next to the notorious (now-demolished) Newgate Prison where prisoners were left to rot (literally) in dark, stinking, underground dungeons, since medieval times. Destroyed in the Great Fire of 1666, it was remodelled several times and the current building dates from 1907. The name, Old Bailey, derives from the lane that runs alongside. The figure of Justice on top of the copper dome overlooks the former site of the public gallows, in use until 1868. Part of the building, including the entrance, was rebuilt after bomb damage in World War II. Inside, the *Old Hall* with its high domed ceiling extolling the virtues of Art, Truth, Justice and Work is one of the most beautiful in London. These courts (some 20 in all) deal with serious crime only and have handled some of the country's most famous modern trials, including Oscar Wilde (1895), Dr Crippen (1910) and William 'Lord Haw-Haw' Joyce (1945). The public can attend current trials in one of the public galleries (join the queue outside for entry).

Museum of London (7 mins)

150 London Wall, EC2
***Tel**: (020) 7600 3699 or 7600 0807 (recorded info); www.museumoflondon.org.uk*
***Open**: Mon–Sat 10am–5.50pm, Sun noon–5.50pm*
***Adm**: free (charges for special exhibitions)*
Gift shop and café
Wheelchair access via lifts in Aldersgate Street
Note: the Museum is being expanded over several years; check the website or phone in advance, as some sections may be temporarily closed

This imaginative museum tells the story of

London from prehistoric times to now, using a mixture of models (including a Viking ship, the Great Fire and a modern terraced street), artefacts and historical documents. Some of the most lively displays are reconstructions and include a Newgate prison cell, a 16th-century grocer's shop, a Victorian pub and a World War II bedroom with a protective cage called a Morrison shelter. The ornate State Coach used at the Lord Mayor's show (second Saturday in November), is parked here the other 364 days of the year.

Club Gascon

57 West Smithfield, EC1A

Tel: (020) 7796 0600

Expensive

This excellent Gascony-influenced restaurant offers an innovative list of rich pickings, quite literally, with foie gras a speciality. Next door the Cellar Gascon offers the same menu but in smaller portions, and prices drop accordingly.

St Bartholomew's Hospital Museum (10 mins)

West Smithfield, EC1 (northwest of the station, entrance through the Henry VIII Gateway);
Tel: (020) 7601 8152
Open*: Tue–Fri 10am–4pm, closed public hols*
Adm*: by donation; Guided tours Friday at 2pm (adults £5, concessions £4, children free)*
Wheelchair access by arrangement

St Bartholomew's Hospital (Barts) is the oldest hospital in London, founded in 1123 by an Augustinian monk, Rahere. Its museum displays a collection showing the history of the hospital and of medicine.

It is best to visit this museum as part of

St Bartholomew's Hospital Museum, West Smithfield

the guided tour, which also takes in the churches of *St Bartholomew the Less and the Great*, the *hospital square*, *North Wing* and *Cloth Fair*. The highlight, seen only on the tour, is James Gibbs' splendid 18th-century Great Hall and staircase, over which hangs Hogarth's two famous 1737 paintings depicting the *Good Samaritan* and *Christ healing the lame man at the Pool of Bethesda* (the models for the figures in the latter are said to have been patients).

You can reach St Bartholomew the Great independently: go along the northerly part of Little Britain – home to many booksellers during the 16th–18th centuries – and you will reach a timber-framed gatehouse, which leads to the church, the only part of Rahere's 12th-century priory that now remains. Only a third of the original building survives after successive demolitions and rebuildings over the years, including wartime bomb damage and a Victorian restoration. The church contains Rahere's tomb from 1405.

BANK

see **Northern Line (Bank branch), p.114**
St Stephen Walbrook p.114, Bank of England Museum p.114, Guildhall p.115, Guildhall Art Gallery p.116, Clockmaker's Company Museum p.117

LIVERPOOL STREET

Broadgate Ice Rink (2 mins)
Broadgate Circle
Tel: (020) 7505 4068
Open: Nov–Mar, Mon–Fri noon–2.30pm, 3.30–5.30pm, also Fri 7–9pm, Sat–Sun 11am–1pm, 2–4pm, 5–7pm
Adm: adults £8, children/concessions £5

This tiny outdoor ice rink was the first in London, and may well have begun what seems now to be a craze (there are winter ice rinks at Somerset House (**see** p.68) and Kew Gardens (**see** p.178), as well as up and down the country). Fairy lights light your way, against a backdrop of modern office buildings and a public square full of contemporary art.

Aurora

Old Great Eastern Hotel, Liverpool Street, EC2

Tel: (020) 7618 7000

Expensive

One of Terence Conrans's better restaurants, located within the finery of the old railway hotel. It's a little bit pricy, but worth it for a treat.

Boisdale

Swedeland Court, 202 Bishopsgate, EC2

Tel: (020) 7283 1763

Open: Mon–Fri 11.30am–midnight

Expensive

There's a wonderful Scottish and game-oriented menu at this unassuming restaurant, with live jazz music and a long list of single malt whiskies.

The Ten Bells

84 Commerical Street, E1

Tel: (020) 7366 1721

Inexpensive

Atmospheric pub that is famous for its association with the Jack the Ripper murders – all his victims were killed within close proximity of here, and one used to ply her trade outside.

Spitalfields Market (4 mins)

Bounded by Brushfield Street, Commercial Street and Lamb Street (exit the station onto Bishopsgate); www.spitalfields.org.uk
Open: *Mon–Fri 11am–3pm, Sun 9.30am–5.30pm*

A vegetable market was founded at Spitalfields in 1682 and today Old Spitalfields is said to be London's most popular market, despite the very apparent threat from developers and the borough council (a glass-and-steel Foster edifice has already been built over half of the original site, and the future of the rest is uncertain at the time of writing). The remaining Victorian structure is host to a lively throng of around 300 stalls and shops, selling food (Wed), clothing (Thu), books and records (third Wed of month) and a multifarious selection of everything including crafts, art, collectables, plus unusual new and second-hand apparel and furniture on Sunday (which is really the best day to go).

Christ Church, Spitalfields (5 mins)

Corner of Fournier Street and Commercial St
Tel: *(020) 7859 3035;*
www.christchurchspitalfields.org
Open: *Tue 11am–4pm and Sun 1–4pm*
www.spitalfieldsfestival.org.uk
Wheelchair accessible

Built in 1714, this is a glorious, enormous English Baroque church designed by Nicholas Hawksmoor. It is one of 50 churches that were commissioned by an act of Parliament in 1711 to impress the Anglican church on the new and increasingly nonconformist populations on the outskirts of London's. The building has undergone a massive restoration since the 1990s and is the focus of events during the Spitalfields classical music festival, held twice a year.

Tower Bridge

The Circle line (1868–84) was designed to connect London's mainline termini. It encompasses zone 1 and runs in tandem with the Metropolitan (1860) and Hammersmith & City lines (1988) from Paddington to Farringdon and the District Line (1868–1902) from Tower Bridge to Edgware Road. The latter continues into the suburbs, see Further Afield, p.176

CIRCLE LINE

NOTTING HILL GATE ■
Portobello Market 52

BAYSWATER ■

PADDINGTON ■■■

EDGWARE ROAD ■ ■ ■

BAKER STREET ■■■ ■
Madame Tussaud's and the
London Auditorium, *see* p.14
Sherlock Holmes Museum,
see p.16

GREAT PORTLAND ST ■

EUSTON SQUARE ■
Percival David Foundation of
Chinese Art, *see* p.53

KING'S CROSS ST PANCRAS ■■■
St Pancras Station, *see* p.110
London Canal Museum,
see p.110

FARRINGDON ■
Smithfield Market 53
Museum of the Order
of St John 54

BARBICAN ■
Barbican Arts Centre 55

● NOTTING HILL GATE

Portobello Market (5 mins)
Portobello Road, W10
Open: *Sat 7am–6pm (antiques); Fri 7am–4pm, Sat 8am–5pm, Sun 9am–4pm (clothes and bric-a-brac); Thu 9am–6pm (organic produce); Mon–Wed 8am–6pm, Thu 9am–1pm, Fri & Sat 7am–7pm (general)*

When the sun is shining, a Saturday morning spent rummaging along Portobello Road is hard to beat. Even if it is raining, there is something so vibrant about this area that rarely fails to lift the spirits. Portobello is actually several markets joined top-to-tail. They stretch for over a mile – begin at the Notting Hill end. Here you find antiques, rugs, paintings (some even genuine) and high prices. Walk down and you are in a bustling fruit and vegetable market. On this stretch there are plenty of trendy cafés and pubs. Further on still, under the Westway flyover, Portobello transforms itself once again to become London's best bric-a-brac market with all manner of collectibles, including antique radios, china, glass and toys, as well as clothes and CDs galore.

● BAKER STREET

see Bakerloo line, p.14
Madame Tussaud's and the London Auditorium p.14, Sherlock Holmes's Museum p.16

Geale's

2 Farmer St, W8

Tel: (020) 7727 7528

Open: Mon–Sat noon–3pm and 6–11pm, Sun 6–10.30pm

Inexpensive

Classy, popular sit-down fish (or oysters) and chips.

Sausage and Mash Café

268 Portobello Road, W10

Tel: (020) 8968 8898

Open: Tue–Sun 11am–10pm

Moderate

Top-notch bangers and mash.

Windsor Castle

114 Campden Hill Road, W8

Tel: (020) 7243 9551

Open: Mon–Sat noon–11pm, Sun noon–10.30pm

Moderate

Pretty walled garden with good pub food and a relaxed atmosphere.

Portobello Market

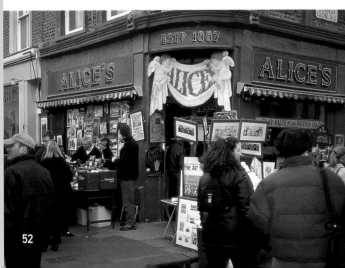

Diwana Bhel Poori House

121 Drummond Street, NW1

Tel: (020) 7387 5556

inexpensive

Lightly spiced but hearty vegetarian food from South India, at bargain prices. The buffet is great value.

Prince Arthur

80–82 Eversholt Street, NW1

Tel: (020) 7387 2165

Moderate

Friendly and comfortable pub serving Thai food.

EUSTON SQUARE

Percival David Foundation of Chinese Art (10 mins)

53 Gordon Square, WC1

Tel: (020) 7387 3909; www.pdfmuseum.org.uk

Open: *Mon–Fri 10.30am–5pm*

Adm: *by donation*

Small gift shop; Wheelchair accessible

All ceramic lovers should visit this museum, which sits quietly on three floors of a converted 19th-century house in Bloomsbury. Sir Percival David, an avid collector and scholar of Chinese ceramics, donated his collection to the University of London in 1952. His collection is the finest in the world outside the Imperial Chinese Collection, and contains exquisite pieces dating from the 10th century onwards.

Delicate shapes and decorations abound; especially lovely are the depictions of grasshoppers and carp; lotus, lilies and blossom; and kingfishers and magpies. The ground floor has a changing themed display drawn from the collection, and the third floor shows highly colourful, later pieces.

KING'S CROSS ST PANCRAS

see **Northern line, p.110**

St Pancras Station p.110, London Canal Museum, p.110

The Eagle

159 Farringdon Road, EC1

Tel: (020) 7837 1353

Moderate

Excellent food from fresh, quality ingredients is served here, in what is reputedly one of the original gastropubs. Very popular, especially in the evening.

FARRINGDON

Smithfield Market (6 mins)

Charterhouse Street, EC1

www.cityoflondon.gov.uk

Open: *Mon–Fri 4am–noon*

Occupying a long, listed Victorian market building, Smithfield Market is one of the most modern meat markets in Europe. It is also one of London's oldest markets, having stood in or near this spot since the 10th century. Its name comes from the 'smooth field' that was once here, where livestock was sold, and tournaments and sports events were held.

Smithfield Market, Charterhouse Street

The livestock market was moved to Islington in 1855. Today there are 44 meat and poultry traders operating here, selling over 85,000 tons of meat a year, plus cheese and delicatessen goods. You'll have to get up early to see the action – but a consolation is that some local pubs are licensed from 6.30am (*see* The Fox and Anchor, *right*), so you'll be able to order a tasty breakfast.

Museum of the Order of St John (7 mins)

St John's Gate, St John's Lane, Clerkenwell, EC1
Tel: *(020) 7324 4070*
www.sja.org.uk/museum
Open: *Mon–Fri 10am–5pm, Sat 10am–4pm,*
Adm: *by donation*
Guided tours of buildings: *Tue, Fri, Sat at 11am and 2.30pm (adults £5, seniors £3.50)*
Gift/book shop; Ground floor and chapter house wheelchair accessible
The Priory of St John of Jerusalem was founded here in the 12th century, and was one of 25 priories in Europe belonging to the Order of St John. In medieval times, the Order was very rich and powerful; however, during the Dissolution of the Monasteries (1536), Henry VIII seized all their property.

The Fox and Anchor

115 Charterhouse Street, EC1

Tel: (020) 7253 5075

Open: Mon–Fri 7am–9pm, closed weekends

Inexpensive

A 19th-century pub near Smithfield Market that enjoys an early licence (it serves English breakfast from 7am), with a lavish tiled façade and attractive Edwardian interior.

Moro

34 Exmouth Market, EC1

Tel: 0871 223 8071

Expensive

Restaurant offering a fusion of Spanish and Middle Eastern fare, in a friendly and relaxed environment.

Today the beautiful 12th-century Norman crypt, 16th-century church and Tudor gatehouse remain. In the reign of Queen Anne the Tudor gatehouse was used as a printers for the 'Gentleman's Magazine'; Samuel Johnson (*see* p.42) was a contributor.

The museum also charts the history of the St John Ambulance brigade, which was launched here in 1877. On display are relics, including pieces of rare armour, from the reign of the Knights Hospitaller on the islands of Malta and Rhodes; there's also a bronze cannon given to the Order by Henry VIII, a 15th-century Flemish altarpiece from the priory church and archaeological exhibits from the priory site.

BARBICAN ⭕

Searcy's

Level 2, Barbican Arts Centre, Silk Street

Tel: (020) 7588 3008

Open: Mon–Fri noon–2.30pm and 5–10.30pm, Sat 5–10.30pm, Sun noon–2.30pm and 5–6.30pm

Expensive

Modern British food in this cheery brasserie. A little expensive but good quality, with a view over the central courtyard.

Barbican Arts Centre (8 mins)
Silk Street, The Barbican, EC2
Tel: (020) 7368 4141; www.barbican.org.uk
Open: Mon–Sat 9am–11pm, Sun and hols noon–11pm; box office open daily 9am–8pm
Restaurant, bars, café; Wheelchair accessible

Opened in 1982, the Barbican is home to the London Symphony Orchestra, the English Chamber Orchestra and the Guildhall School of Music and Drama. It also has three cinemas, an art gallery, several bars and a couple of restaurants, not to mention the shops, residential high-rise flats and the underground car park.

Londoners don't really like the Barbican – but they come for the quality of the performances (dance, theatre, music), the world-class concerts and exhibitions and, during the summer, the terrace with its pond and benches, which is a popular drinking spot, especially when there is a free jazz band playing.

LIVERPOOL STREET ⭕

see Central line, p.48
Broadgate Ice Rink p.48, Spitalfields Market p.48, Christ Church, Spitalfields p.49

⬤ ALDGATE

St Katharine Cree (5 mins)

86 Leadenhall Street, EC3
Tel: *(020) 7283 5733*
www.stkatharinecree.org
Open: *Mon–Fri 10.30am–4pm*

St Katharine's dates from 1628–31 (an earlier church was built in the 13th century) and escaped both the Great Fire (1666) and any serious bombing in World War II, so its original interior is virtually intact. The design is attributed to Edmund Kinsman, an employee of Inigo Jones and it has plenty of famous associations: the organ dates from 1686 and has been played by Purcell, Wesley and Handel; the altar table is attributed to Robert Adam and, it is said, the painter Hans Holbein was buried in the crypt of the earlier church. The splendid plaster ceiling shows the arms of 17 City Livery Companies. The tracery in the impressive east rose window reflects the wheel upon which St Catherine escaped torture and is said to be modelled on a window from old St Paul's (**see** p.44).

Petticoat Lane Market (5 mins)

Middlesex Street, EC1
Open: *Sun 9am–2pm*

Don't look for Petticoat Lane on the map. It isn't there and hasn't existed since 1830, when the Victorians decided to change its name for reasons of delicacy. Petticoat Lane is at the heart of what was once the city's rag trade and although you won't see too many petticoats, you'll find other underwear, shirts, socks, coats, jeans and hats. If you are after a good-quality leather jacket at a rock-bottom price, head for the top end of the market near Aldgate East Tube. The crammed streets off the main drag offer all kinds of bric-a-brac, furniture, jewellery, cycles, books, CDs and assorted junk. (A word of caution: not everything you find here has been honestly acquired.) If you are feeling peckish, there are plenty of places to pick up a bagel or salt-beef sandwich.

Café Spice Namaste

16 Prescot Street, E1

Tel: (020) 7488 9242

Open: Mon–Fri noon–3pm, 6.15–10.30pm, Sat 6.15–10pm

Expensive

Innovative Indian restaurant in a former Victorian law court. Home-made Indian pickles can be bought to take home. Tends to fill up with City types during the week.

Whitechapel Art Gallery (2 mins)

80–82 Whitechapel High Street, E1
Tel: *(020) 7522 7878/7888; www.whitechapel.org*
Open: *Tue–Sun 11am–6pm, Thu 11am–9pm*
Adm: *free (except for some exhibitions)*
Gift shop and café-bar; Wheelchair accessible

This Art Nouveau building was completed
in 1897 and, from its early days, exhibited
contemporary art. Today it is an important
international art venue, hosting programmes
that are at the cutting edge of modern art.
There are also films, talks and other art-
related events. A £10 million expansion is
planned and due to be completed in 2007.

Brick Lane Market (5 mins)

*Brick Lane (north of railway bridge), Bethnal
Green Road, Cygnet Street, Grimsby Street,
Sclater Street E1; Bacon Street, Cheshire Street, E2*
Open: *Sun 8am–1pm*

In the 16th century they used to make bricks
here. These days, it is alive with cheap
Indian restaurants, stores selling brightly
coloured saris or Indian sweets and small-
scale textile factories. On Sunday mornings,
it becomes one of London's busiest markets,
attracting a wide variety of Londoners who
come early looking for bric-à-brac, clothes
and food. It's fairly scruffy but fun to poke
about in, especially among the more
established covered stalls halfway down.

Brick Lane is not as cheap as it once was, but there is still the chance – unlike at Portobello Market – that you may pick up a genuine antique for pounds if not pennies.

⬤ TOWER HILL

Tower of London (6 mins)

Tower Hill, EC3
***Tel**: 0870 756 6060; www.hrp.org.uk*
***Open**: Mar–Oct Tue–Sat 9am–6pm, Sun–Mon 10am–6pm; Nov–Feb Tue–Sat 9am–5pm, Sun–Mon 10am–5pm; last adm 1 hour before closing*
***Adm**: adults £13.50, concessions £10.50, children £9, families £37.50 (£1 off if tickets bought by phone or online; joint tickets with Hampton Court or Kensington Palace available)*
Café and restaurant; 5 shops
Very limited wheelchair access

William the Conqueror built the White Tower as a fortress after he invaded England in 1066 to protect himself from English rebels. It was further strengthened by successive monarchs, to include two additional towers, outer walls and a moat (now dry). As well as keeping people out, the Tower

The White Tower, the Tower of London

has proved useful at keeping them in. Among the prisoners brought here through Traitor's Gate were Anne Boleyn, Katherine Howard (Wives 2 and 5 respectively of Henry VIII), Lady Jane Grey, Sir Thomas More, Sir Walter Raleigh and Guy Fawkes. Some of these were executed on Tower Green, where the squawking ravens are all that remain of the menagerie introduced by Henry III. It included lions, leopards, a polar bear (kept on a chain so it could fish in the Thames) and an elephant; the animals were moved to London Zoo in 1834.

The Tower is also home to the *Crown Jewels*, which glitter behind bulletproof glass; you view them from a moving walkway, which takes you past gently. Among the priceless collection of baubles are the Royal Sceptre, the Imperial State Crown (which includes 2,800 diamonds and the Black Prince's ruby, reputedly worn by Henry V at the Battle of Agincourt in 1415), and the 530-carat Cullinan stone, the world's largest cut diamond. Though you can take a spooky subterranean ride on the Tower Hill Pageant, the best way to learn more is to take a free tour. These leave every half hour from the Middle Tower and are conducted by one of the 38 resident Yeoman Warders. A fact-packed walk round the principal sights, they have the additional benefit of letting you talk personally to one of the famous Beefeaters (so-called because of their daily 2lb ration of meat) who have been faithfully guarding the Tower since 1458.

Tower Bridge Museum (10 mins)

Exhibition, tel: (020) 7403 3761;
Bridge opening times, tel: (020) 7940 3984
www.towerbridge.org.uk
Open: *Apr–Sep daily 10am–5.30pm (last adm),*
Oct–Mar daily 9.30am–5pm (last adm); last
adm 1 hour before closing
Adm: *adults £5.50, concessions £4.25, 5–15s £3*
Wheelchair accessible

Mock-gothic rather than the real thing, Tower Bridge was unveiled in 1894, and was innovative for being constructed around a steel frame. Although a little pricy, the tour is worth it as you are taken back in time by Harry Stoner, an animatronic construction worker. Interactive displays and the occasional appearance of the ghost of Horace Jones, the bridge's architect who died before the work was complete, only add to the fun. The tour takes you up to the elevated walkways that run along the top, offering a grand view up and down the river, and ends in the engine room where you can see the gleaming steam pumps used to lift the decks until 1976. The bridge is not raised as often as it once was, but the bascules still rise at least once a day.

Tower Bridge

⬤ MONUMENT

The Monument (0 mins)
Monument Street, EC3 (just outside station)
***Tel**: (020) 7626 2717; www.cityoflondon.gov.uk*
***Open**: daily 10am–6pm, last adm 5.30pm;*
***Adm**: adults £2, under-16s £1.50 (joint ticket with Tower Bridge £5.50/3.50)*

On 2 September 1666, in the early hours of the morning, a fire broke out at Farynor's bakery in Pudding Lane. It was a windy night and sparks soon set fire to the nearby Star Inn and, from there, spread through the entire neighbourhood. By morning London Bridge and 300 houses were ablaze. Four days later, when the fire was finally under control, 13,200 houses, 44 livery halls and 87 churches (including the old St Paul's – **see** p.44) had gone up in smoke. Amazingly, only 18 people had perished.

The Monument, designed by Christopher Wren, topped by a flaming bronze urn, commemorates these events. At 61m (202ft) – the exact distance from here to the bakery on Pudding Lane – it was the world's tallest isolated stone column when it was erected in 1671. A stiff climb (311 steps) takes you to the gallery at the top where you get a fine view of rooftop London, only partly spoiled by the office buildings crowding round. The bas-relief on the pedestal bears an allegorical design with Charles II standing majestically in a Roman garb and Restoration wig combination, instructing his entourage to aid the distressed and rebuild the city.

St Magnus the Martyr (3 mins)
Lower Thames Street, EC3
Open: *Tue–Fri 10am–4pm, Sun 10am–1pm*
Adm: *by donation; recitals most Tues at 1pm*

St Magnus the Martyr

This marvellous Wren church once stood at the north end of the old London Bridge, the only bridge that crossed the Thames until 1750 (**see** p.100), which shows how important it once was. The church was originally founded around 1100 on land reclaimed from the Thames by the Romans (a fragment of Roman wharf sits in the entrance porch). In medieval times, St Magnus's Corner was where notices were read and punishments, such as hangings, were meted out; 500 years later it was one of the first casualties in the Great Fire; the clock on the tower (1700) was a London landmark until the 1920s when it became half-hidden by the Art Deco block next door. T.S. Eliot famously summed up this church in his long poem *The Waste Land*, describing it as an 'inexplicable splendour of Ionian white and gold'. The interior is magnificent with its contrast between the wooden 17th-century pulpit and altarpiece, white washed walls and gilded ionic columns, figures, ceiling and sword-rests. A visit after the Sunday morning service is recommended, when the incense-filled interior renders a hallowed atmosphere.

Old Billingsgate Fish Market (6 mins)
Lower Thames Street; Closed to the public

> *'There stript, fair Rhetoric*
> *languish'd on the ground;*
> *His blunted arms by sophistry are borne,*
> *And shameless Billingsgate her robes adorn.'*

Alexander Pope, *The Dunciad*

Old Billingsgate Fish Market

The fishwives and porters of Billingsgate were well-known for their ribald tongues and Pope was one of many in the 17th century who condemned them for it.

Until 11982, there had been a market here since the 11th century – it was exclusively for fish from 1698. The new market is now on the Isle of Dogs and covers 14 acres. The current Renaissance building (with fishy detailing) dates from 1877 and has recently been refurbished by Richard Rogers. To see the building from the riverside, walk east around St Magnus the Martyr down to the river, turn left and follow the path.

Leadenhall Market (8 mins)
Gracechurch Street, EC2
www.cityoflondon.gov.uk
Open: Mon–Fri 7am–4pm

North of the station, this market was established in the 15th century for 'foreigners', meaning people from outside London, to sell poultry, grain, eggs, butter and cheese. The name comes from the lead-roofed mansion whose estate covered this area, and which, along with parts of the market, was destroyed in the Great Fire (1666). The market was rebuilt and expanded around three courtyards: the Beef Market, selling leather and wool; the Green Yard, selling lamb, mutton and veal; and a yard for herbs, fruit and vegetables, though fish,

Simpson's Tavern

Ball Court, 38 Cornhill, EC3

Tel: (020) 7626 9985

Open: Mon–Fri 11am–11pm

Moderate

This chophouse tries to take you back to what dining was like 200 years ago, with steak and kidney pies, chops and steamed puddings.

Williamson's Tavern

1 Groveland Court, off Bow Lane, EC4

Tel: (020) 7248 628

Inexpensive

A pub that was once the Lord Mayor's residence (before Mansion House was built), with tastefully decorated wooden interiors. Serves decent typical pub food.

Leadenhall Market,
Gracechurch Street

The Lamb Tavern
*Leadenhall Market,
EC3*
Tel: (020) 7626 2454
Inexpensive
Old City boozer in
the atmospheric
covered Leadenhall
market. Famous for
its hot roast beef
baguettes – but
avoid office lunch
hour if you can.

poultry and cheese continued to be sold.

The present highly decorated wrought-iron and glass arcaded structure was built in 1881 by Horace Jones, architect of Old Billingsgate and Smithfield markets. It's a busy and popular weekday haunt: there are still a few shops selling fish, meat, cheese and fresh produce, but smart cafés and clothes shops are also popular. Richard Rogers' famous inside-out Lloyds Building is right next to the market, in Lime Street.

MANSION HOUSE ⬤

St Mary Aldermary (3 mins)
Watling Street, EC4
Tel: (020) 7248 4906;
www.stmaryaldermary.co.uk
Open: Mon–Fri 11am–3pm
Adm: by donation

Along with another 50 City churches, St Mary Aldermary was rebuilt by Christopher Wren after the Great Fire of 1666. It was lucky in that its foundations and parts of the walls, as well as the base of the tower (*c.*1510), survived. St Mary Aldermary is particularly famous for its spectacular fan-vaulted ceiling, which is likely to have been copied from the earlier church.

St Mary-le-Bow (4 mins)

Cheapside, EC2
Tel: *(020) 7248 5139; www.stmarylebow.co.uk*
Open: *Mon–Thu 7.30am–6pm, Fri 6.30am–4pm*
Bell ringing: see website for details
Lunchtime concerts: usually Thu 1.05pm

St Mary-le-Bow's bells are famous from the 'Oranges and Lemons' nursery rhyme ('I do not know, says the great bell of Bow'), and for calling Dick Whittington back when he stopped at Highgate (*see* p.184).

The church was originally founded by the Normans but was destroyed in the Great Fire and rebuilt by Sir Christopher Wren who modelled it on the Roman Basilica of Constantine. It was the most expensive of his rebuildings, costing around £15,600, and is most famous for its Classical steeple, topped by a 3-m (9-ft) weather vane supporting a flying golden dragon (1674). The balcony is an historical feature; an earlier one collapsed in 1331 sending Queen Philippa and her ladies to the ground. From the 14th century St Mary-le-Bow rang out the curfew, and in the 16th century a large bell was given to ring out a 'retreat from work'. This probably gave rise to the belief that true cockneys are born only within earshot of Bow Bells. The original peal (and most of the church) was bombed in 1941; the church was restored from 1956 to 1962.

Mansion House (5 mins)

Victoria Street
Open: *by appointment to organized groups*

This is the official home of the Lord Mayor of the City of London, who is responsible for what happens within the Square Mile

Designed by George Dance the Elder, Mansion House is a magnificent Palladian structure dating from 1752. It is used as offices and for official functions; the Egyptian Hall is famous for being modelled on Roman dining halls in Egypt. The pediment shows an allegorical scene: the female warrior-like 'London' is in the centre, stamping down 'Envy' and bringing in 'Plenty', to her left. On her right stands a

The Place Below

St Mary le Bow

Cheapside, EC2

Tel: (020) 7329 0789; www.theplacebelow.co.uk

Open: Mon–Fri 7.30am–3.30pm

Inexpensive

Light vegetarian breakfasts and lunches using fresh ingredients, served within the Norman crypt of the church. In good weather there is outdoor seating in the churchyard.

Mansion House

cupid with a Liberty Cap and a sea god representing the Thames. Today the building is hemmed in by Progress – in the form of newer buildings and traffic.

TEMPLE

Temple station is only open Mon–Sat; Sun: use Blackfriars or Embankment.

The name of this station derives from the nearby **Inns of Court** (*see* p.40), **Inner Temple** and **Middle Temple**, which sit on the site of a monastery built by the Knights Templar in the 12th century. All that remains is the church (*see* below), but a walk along Inner Temple Lane will take you to the Inn's 17th-century gateway, topped by a timber-frame building rated as the best of its type in London, which contains Prince Henry's Room (*see* p.70). Samuel Johnson (*see* p.42), used to lived at No.1.

Middle Temple Lane has an equally fine 17th-century gatehouse, with a set of marvellous overhanging buildings behind, which are supported by iron posts. If you are lucky you may see *Middle Temple Hall*, on Fountain Court (ask for permission in the Treasury Office, on Middle Temple Lane), which dates from 1573 and has a double hammerbeam roof, oak panelling, royal portraits, Elizabethan suits of armour and a table made from a single oak, said to be a donation from Elizabeth I.

St Clement Danes (5 mins)
Strand, WC2
***Tel**: (020) 7242 8282*
***Open**: daily 8am–4.30pm; **Adm**: by donation*

This magnificent church sits on an island in the centre of the busy Strand thoroughfare, close to the Royal Courts of Justice. It was built by Sir Christopher Wren in 1681 after the previous church, built in stone at the beginning of the 11th century, and which survived the Great Fire of London in 1666, was found to be largely unsafe. Inside, a plaque commemorates the seat of Samuel

Johnson, who was a regular parishioner in the 18th century. A list of the former rectors includes William Webb-Ellis, who was the first to flout the rules of football by taking the ball under his arm – thus inventing 'Rugby football'. Also, take a close look at the mahogany pews: these are telescopic and will extend to seat an extra 10 people.

After bombs destroyed the interior of the church in 1941, members of the RAF and the Commonwealth and Allied Air Forces made a large contribution towards reconstruction; it is now the central church for the Royal Air Force. The church is also associated with the nursery rhyme 'Oranges and Lemons' – although St Clement Eastcheap is more likely to be the church in the rhyme as it stands near wharves where shipments of citrus fruits were once unloaded.

Interior of St Mary le Strand

St Mary le Strand (6 mins)

Strand, WC2; www.stmarylestrand.org
***Open**: Mon–Fri 11am–4pm, Sun 10am–3pm*
***Adm**: by donation*
***Music recitals**: Wed at 1.05pm, except during Lent (see website for details), tickets from information desk in Seamen's Hall on the day*

This slender, elegant Baroque church was built in 1714–17 by James Gibbs. It was one of the first to be built after the Fifty Churches Act of 1711, which aimed to combat a rise of non-conformism and general unruliness in London's suburbs. Even more marooned than its neighbour, St Clement Danes, it sits in the middle of the road, and has been justifiably likened to a barque, majestically sailing away from the City through a sea of traffic. The interior is wonderful, with an ornate coffered ceiling with *trompe-l'oeil* disortion, and marvelous blue postwar and Victorian stained- and clear-glass windows. This was one of Poet Laureate Sir John Betjeman's favourite churches, and in 1977 he launched an appeal for it to be restored. Indeed, Betjeman admired Gibbs' work so much that he addressed him in a poem:

*'There's nothing quite so grand
As the Baroque of your chapel of
St Mary in the Strand'.*

Somerset House (6 mins)

Strand, WC2
Tel: *(020) 7845 4600;*
www.somerset-house.org.uk
Open: *daily 10am–6pm;* **Adm**: *free*
Café, restaurants, bar (in summer) oshop;
Guided tours: *first Sat of month (exc. public hols) at 1.30pm and 3.45pm (free),*
Ice-skating rink: *open Nov–Jan daily 10am–10pm (tel: 0870 166 0423, book well in advance);*
Learning Centre: *Sat workshops 2pm–3.30pm (adm free) ages 6–12; 'Art Start' first Thu of month, 2pm–3.30pm (adm free) for under-5s; school holiday and other seasonal activities*
Wheelchair accessible

This Georgian building was built in the 1770s after the first Somerset House, a Tudor palace built by the Duke of Somerset in the mid-16th century (and which a 17th-century advert claims as the first English building to have parquet flooring), was knocked down. For many years, it was used to house public records but, more recently, it became home to three great art collections, the **Courtauld**, **Hermitage** and **Gilbert Collections** (**see** below), and its courtyard cleared to make a way for a piazza with orchestrated fountains in summer and an ice rink in winter. In summer there is also a programme of live music, both popular and classical. A daily programme of talks, lectures, courses and workshops linked to each gallery are run for adults and children.

Courtauld Institute Gallery

Tel: *(020) 7848 2526; www.courtauld.ac.uk*
Open: *daily 10am–6pm, last adm 5.15pm;*
Adm: *adults £5, concessions £4, students and under-18s free; joint adm with the Hermitage Rooms, £8/7; free adm Mon 10am–2pm except bank holidays*
Café and gift shop; Wheelchair accessible

The Courtauld has a stunning collection of Impressionist and Post-Impressionist paintings, including works by Manet, Monet, Gauguin, Pissarro, Renoir, Van Gogh, Cézanne and Modigliani. There are also 32 works by Rubens, a Botticelli *Trinity* and gouaches by Rouault. This is a gem.

The Admiralty

Somerset House, Strand, WC2

Tel: (020) 7845 4646

Open: Mon–Sat noon–2.45pm and 6–10.45pm

Expensive

Modern European cuisine served in the beautiful surroundings of Somerset House.

The courtyard at Somerset house

Hermitage Rooms

Tel: (020) 7845 4630;
www.hermitagerooms.com
Open: daily 10am–6pm (last adm 5.15pm)
Adm adults £5, concessions £4, under-16s free;
joint adm with Courtauld Gallery £8/7; timed
tickets tel: 0870 906 3765 or from
www.firstcalltickets.com (£1 booking fee)
Gift shop; Wheelchair accessible

The State Hermitage Museum in St
Petersburg holds one of the world's
finest art collections but, despite 10km
of galleries at the Winter Palace, there is
not enough space to display everything.
Since 2001, some of it has been shown
here in five small rooms designed to re-
create the interiors of the Palace on a
smaller scale and decorated with
marquetry floors, chandeliers and textiles.
So far its temporary exhibitions, which
combine *objets* from the Hermitage with
art from other collections, have proved an
enormous hit – hence the timed tickets,
which you should book in advance.

Gilbert Collection

Tel: (020) 7420 9400
www.gilbert-collection.org.uk
Open: daily 10am–6pm, last adm 5.15pm
Adm: adults £5, concessions £4, under-18s free
Gift shop; Wheelchair accessible.

A treasure trove gifted by Londoner Sir Arthur
Gilbert in 1949, the collection comprises 17
galleries of beautiful English gold- and

silverware, Roman and italian mosaics, miniatures and much besides. An informative audio guide is included in the price.

Temple Church (7 mins)

Inner Temple Lane
Tel: (020) 7353 3470; www.templechurch.com
Open: Wed–Sat 8.30am–4pm
Adm: by donation
Organ recitals: Wed at 1.15–1.45pm (free)
Wheelchair accessible

If you've read Dan Brown's best-seller, *The Da Vinci Code*, you'll know of this church, tucked away down Inner Temple Lane. Temple church is in two parts. The *Round Church* was built in 1185 by the Knights Templar, an order of 'soldier monks' that was founded to protect pilgrims on their way to and from the Holy Land. Its shape was intended to reflect that of either the Holy Sepulchre or the Dome of the Rock (nobody is quite sure), both in Jerusalem. The *Chancel*, which has outward-leaning columns, was built in 1240. There are nine life-size stone effigies of medieval knights in the Round church, several dating from the 13th century.

Temple Church

Prince Henry's Room (8 mins)

First floor, 17 Fleet Street EC4
Tel: (020) 8294 1158; www.cityoflondon.gov.uk
Open: Mon–Fri 11am–2pm
Adm: by donation

Little of London remains that predates the Great Fire of 1666, but this is one of the

Medieval tombs of Knight Templar, Temple Church, Inner Temple Lane

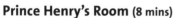

Seven Stars

53 Carey Street, WC2

Tel: (020) 7242 8521

Open: Mon–Sat 11am–11pm (food served noon–7.30pm)

Inexpensive

Built in 1602, this is one of the few buildings to survive the Great Fire. It has a snug bar and open fire, and is furnished with settles. Often full of characters from the nearby Inns and Royal Courts, with mischevious staff.

Champagne Charlie's

The Arches, Villiers Street, WC2

Tel: (020) 7930 7737

Moderate

Cellar ale and port house serving hearty favourites such as rib-eye steak, seared swordfish and charcoal grilled chicken. Try a tankard of Davy's Old Wallop.

Gordon's

47 Villiers Street, WC2

Tel: (020) 7930 1408

Moderate

A characterful cellar wine bar, with sputtering candles, speciality wines and simple food. The terrace outside has seating in summer.

notable exceptions (the fire was stopped just yards east of here). A Jacobean half-timbered house, Prince Henry's Room was built, it is thought, in 1611 to honour Henry, James I's eldest son, who had just become the Prince of Wales. Some original oak panelling and all of the remarkable Jacobean plaster ceiling, one of the best examples of its kind in London (in the centre are the Prince of Wales' feathers, and the initials 'PH'), are still intact. The room is now used to house a small collection devoted to the 17th-century diarist Samuel Pepys, which includes various extracts from his diary, a letter written by him and a pair of his spectacles.

EMBANKMENT

The Romans were the first to try to reclaim land from the Thames but it wasn't until 1868 that work began on the Victoria Embankment, a task that took six years. The Chelsea and Albert Embankments were constructed further west. The avenues of plane trees and the lamp posts with dolphins curled at the base are typical of them all.

Golden Jubilee Bridge (1 min)
Wheelchair accessible (via lifts)

Most Londoners will agree that this bridge is a wonderful addition to central London's riverside, providing a convenient link between the West End and the revitalized South Bank (*see* p.23), and giving superb views of London's riverside buildings. Opened in 2002–3, it replaced the decaying old Hungerford footbridge. The bridge is at its best lit up at night, with iridescent beams shining along the masts and walkways

Embankment Gardens (1 min)
Victoria Embankment
Open: *daily 7.30am–dusk*

These pretty gardens, south of the Strand (which means 'Beach' – a word introduced

Golden Jubilee bridge,
Victoria Embankment

by the Vikings), were formed from reclaimed land. Opened in 1870, they are filled with monuments to statesmen (such as Prime Minister, William Gladstone), war heroes (General Charles Gordon, 'Gordon of Khartoum') and other historical figures, including the Scottish poet Robert Burns. The most interesting feature is the 17th-century Water Gate in the northwest corner – once the Duke of Buckingham's entrance to the Thames from York House, which was nearby. The gate is on its original site – but is now 100m (328ft) from the water. In summer, there are free lunchtime concerts.

Cleopatra's Needle (3 mins)
Victoria Embankment

Just across the road from Embankment Gardens (you can approach it from the gardens or the road), this granite Egyptian obelisk stands right on the Thames and is 18m (60ft) high. It was given to the British in 1819 by the Turkish Viceroy of Egypt, Mohammed Ali; 58 years later an English engineer, John Dixon, figured out how to get it back to London using a cylindrical iron pontoon. Both pontoon and obelisk were nearly lost on the journey in a gale that claimed several lives, but it finally reached London in 1878.

The obelisk dates from about 1475 BC and originally sat at Heliopolis. It shows carved dedications to gods and cartouches for Pharoahs Tuthmosis III, Ramses II and Cleopatra. An assortment of items was buried underneath the Needle when it was erected: the morning newspapers, a set of

Ship and Shovell

1-3 Craven Passage, WC2

Tel: (020) 7839 1311

Open: Mon-Sat

11am-11pm

Inexpensive

Pleasant pub in two halves, each with its own bar, serving a good selection of beers.

coins, a razor and a box of pins, four bibles in various languages, a railway guide and photographs of the most beautiful women of the time. Whoever – or whatever – discovers them in 3,500 years time will surely be intrigued.

WESTMINSTER

see Jubilee line, p.90

ST JAMES'S PARK

Inn the Park

St James's Park, SW1

Tel: (020) 7451 9999; www.innthepark.co.uk

Open: summer daily 8am–11pm; winter Mon–Fri 8am–11pm, Sat 9am–10pm, Sun 9am–5pm

Moderate

An eaterie in the middle of the park, within a modern wooden building that has indoor or al fresco seating. Fresh, modern, British-sourced food, for breakfast, lunch, afternoon tea or dinner; or, you can just have a drink.

St James's Park (3 mins)

The Mall, SW1
Tel: (020) 7930 1793; www.royalparks.gov.uk
Open: daily dawn–dusk
Adm: free

Built on top of a former leper colony, St James's is now the prettiest park in London, with tall trees, a graceful stretch of water and fine views of Buckingham Palace (*see* below). It was originally marshland but was drained in the 15th century to create the deer park for St James's Palace. In the 17th century the park had several aviaries (hence Birdcage Walk, which runs along its west side) and today its lake is home to over 20 different kinds of bird, including pelicans. A playground (with sandpit) and an upmarket café-restaurant (Inn the Park) make this a good stop-off point if you have children. At night, coloured spotlights across the waters make the views even more magical.

Guards' Museum (5 mins)

Wellington Barracks
(entrance on Birdcage Walk), SW1
Tel: (020) 7414 3428
Open: daily 10am–4pm (last adm 3.30pm);
Adm: adults £2, concessions £1, under-16s free
Toy Soldier Centre open Sat–Thu 10am–4pm, tel: (020) 7976 0850, www.mklmodels.co.uk
Wheelchair accessible

St James's Park

This museum tells the story of the men who have served in the royal Foot Guards (the ones you see in the Changing of the Guard ceremony at Buckingham Palace, *see* below for times), since the Civil War. On display are uniforms, weaponry, medals and paintings. The Guards Toy Soldier Centre is one of the best places in London to buy toy soldiers, both antique and new.

Buckingham Palace (11 mins)

The Mall, SW1
***Tel**: (020) 7766 7300; www.royal.gov.uk*
***Open**: Aug–Sep daily 9.30am–6.30pm (timed tickets)*
***Adm**: adult £13.50, under-17s £7 (under-5s free), concessions £11.50, family £34*
State Apartments: Aug–Sep; buy tickets at ticket office at Canada Gate in Green Park (open 9am–6pm) or in advance by phone or online (£1 fee per ticket)
Wheelchair accessible through separate entrance; please contact ticket sales staff

Guard outside Buckingham Palace, The Mall

Buckingham Palace is something of a newcomer in terms of royal residences. Originally built in 1703 for the Duke of Buckingham, George III bought it in 1762, renaming it the 'King's House'. His spendthrift son George IV knocked it down and hired the architect John Nash to turn it into a palace. Nash produced a grand plan for a vast three-sided building with a triumphal arch (the Marble Arch, which now stands at the top of Park Lane, *see* p.31). After George died in 1830, Parliament, shocked at the mounting cost, sacked Nash

*36 Buckingham
Palace Road, London,
SW1W 0RE*

020 7834 7761

*Open: Mon-Fri for
meals
12am–2.30pm and
5.30pm–10pm*

*Wine Bar open 12am
–11pm*

Moderate

Tiles has proved
reliable and
consistently
providing an
inexpensive wine
list with good food
to match. Seating is
available outside

and gave the work to Edward Blore, a
plodding but efficient architect who finished
the job as cheaply as he could. The final
result was a disaster with stinking lavatories,
windows that wouldn't open, bells that
wouldn't ring and doors that wouldn't shut.
Despite calling it a 'disgrace to the country'
Queen Victoria made it her home in 1837
following her accession and it has been the
monarch's official residence ever since.

Eighteen State rooms are open to the
public when the Queen is away (Aug–Sep),
including the *Throne Room*, the *State
Dining Room* and the *Music room* (where
Princess Diana allegedly tap danced while
Elton John played the piano). The *Picture
Gallery* has hundreds of paintings on its
walls, including works by Poussin, Claude
Lorraine, Frans Hals and Rubens.

Changing of the Guard
*Apr-Jun daily 11.30am; rest of the year on
alternate days, see website for more details*

The guard, consisting of three officers and
40 soldiers of the Foot Guard (fewer if the
Queen is not at home), all wearing their
signature red coats and bearskin hats,
march from Wellington Barracks on
Birdcage Walk, along the Mall to
Buckingham palace to take over duty.

Buckingham Palace,
The Mall

Queen's Gallery (12 mins)

Buckingham Gate, SW1
*Tel: (020) 7766 7301 (tickets)/7323
(information); www.royal.gov.uk*
Open: daily 10am–5.30pm, timed tickets only
*Adm: adult £7.50, seniors and students £6,
under-17s £4, under-5s free, family (2+3) £19*
Wheelchair accessible

Just around the south side of Buckingham
Palace is the Queen's Gallery – seven rooms
in which are displayed items from the
Royal Collection. This constitutes a huge
collection of art and treasures (paintings,
jewellery, ceramics, furniture, clocks, silver
and gold, sculpture, books...), which has
been shaped by British kings and queens
over the last 500 years. It is one of the
finest collections in the world, and today is
held in trust by the Queen for the nation. A
programme of exhibitions is held, alongside
changing exhibits from the Collection;
themes include 'Dutch Paintings of the
Golden Age' and 'Canaletto in Venice'.

VICTORIA

see **Victoria line, p.172**

Royal Mews p.172, Westminster Cathedral p.173

SLOANE SQUARE

Named for an 18th-century Lord of Chelsea
Manor, Sir Hans Sloane (whose collections
formed the basis for the British Museum
(*see* p.37), the square is dominated on the
west side by the department store **Peter
Jones**, opened in 1877 by a Welsh draper's
assistant, where you can find everything
practical that you might ever need, from
candles to sportswear. Next to the station
is the **Royal Court Theatre** (tel: (020) 7565
5000, www.royalcourt theatre.com),
famous for new and groundbreaking
theatre, and on the north side is **Sloane
Street**, which takes you up to
Knightsbridge (*see* p.147). Sloane Street is
the place in London for couture fashion and

El Blason

*8–9 Blacklands
Terrace, SW3*

Tel: (020) 7823 7383

Expensive

Authentic and
friendly Spanish
tapas bar, with a
lively atmosphere.

chic luxury goods and, even if you aren't buying, it's fun to window shop. On the west side you'll find Prada, Giorgio Armani, MaxMara, Dior, Gianfranco Ferre, Marni, Fendi, Gucci; and on the east side: Chanel, Yves Saint Laurent, Pucci, Valentino, Dolce & Gabbana, Bulgari, Hermes, Versace, Cartier, Louis Vuitton, Escada, Lalique and at the end, Harvey Nichols, the most *à la mode* department store in London (**see** p.147).

King's Road, SW3 (2 mins)

The King's Road is so named because it once belonged to King Charles II who used it to go to and from Hampton Court. George III also found it a pleasure to use on his way to Kew (**see** p.178). The road wasn't made a public right of way until as late as 1830. Over a century later it became a hotbed for the youthful, creative energy that swept British music and fashion in the 1960s.

Today the King's Road is still a vibrant, stylish place to shop, although at a more moderately priced level than in Sloane Street. As well as high-street familiars, you will find individual boutiques, of which the following is a brief rundown. Beginning at the Sloane Square end, on the south side: Oliver Sweeney (no.29) sells men's shoes and accessories; R Soles (no.109a) is famous for cowboy boots; the Harley Davidson store (no.125) sells leathers and accessories; Antiquarius (nos.131–41) comprises 70 antiques dealers selling paintings, furniture, porcelain and jewellery; Daisy & Tom (no.181) specializes in children's books, clothes, toys and accessories; Steinberg and Tolkien is famous for antique clothing, which includes 'vintage'

Big Easy

332–4 King's Road, SW3

Tel: (020) 7352 4071

Moderate

Great for perfect, freshly cooked steaks, burgers and ribs in generous portions.

Bluebird Club and Dining Rooms

350 King's Road, SW3

Tel: (020) 7559 1129

Open: Mon–Sat noon–3pm and 6–11pm, Sun noon–3.30pm and 6–10.30pm

Expensive

Run by Tom, son of Terence Conran, the restaurant has understated glamour.

Sloane Square

couture and designer labels (no.193); Green & Stone (no.259) sells artists' materials, and claims it is one of the oldest shops of its kind in London; Designers Guild (no.277) has contemporary interior furnishings, textiles, accessories and a café; Rococo Chocolates (no.321) is run by the founder of the Chocolate Society, and full of tantalizing delights for connoisseurs of proper chocolate.

Coming back up the road on the north side, you'll find: World's End (no.430), the shop belonging to that eccentric m'lady of fashion design, Vivienne Westwood; Bluebird (No.350), Terence Conran's food emporium, set in an old Art Deco garage, with a Conran Shop next door selling his lifestyle philosophy of modern design; Brora (no.344), for Scottish cashmere woollens and tweeds; Heals (no.234), for cool interior furnishings and accessories; and Diesel (no.72), for hip urban men's and women's fashion. Also of interest is Chelsea Farmers' Market, just off the King's Road on Sydney Street. You won't find any muddy wellies here – this is possibly the classiest farmer's market around, with rather twee but appealing craft shops and cafés.

Royal Hospital, Chelsea (12 mins)

Royal Hospital Road, SW3
***Tel**: (020) 7881 5204*
www.chelsea-pensioners.org.uk
***Open**: Mon–Sat 10am–noon and 2–4pm, Sun 2–4pm (closed all bank hols and Sun Oct–Mar)*
***Adm**: free; Gift shop, Wheelchair accessible*
Buses from Sloane Square 19, 21, C1

The existence of a home for veteran soldiers is all down to King Charles II who, after the Restoration (1660) and inspired by the *Hôtel des Invalides in Paris*, decided that that some provision had to be made for old and injured soldiers. Until then, religious foundations had looked after the casualties of war. Charles authorized the building of a Royal Hospital in 1681 and appointed Sir Christopher Wren as architect. Cashflow held things up but the hospital finally opened in 1692 with 476 resident pensioners.

The Royal Hospital

Wren designed the buildings around three courtyards; the middle one, the Figure Court, has a golden statue of Charles II at its centre. The pensioners are the stars; while in residence they often wear the hospital's uniform, which is navy blue with a peaked cap bearing the initials 'RH'. Better-known are their scarlet dress uniform and tricorn hats, which they wear on ceremonial occasions.

On a visit you can see some of the interior, including the panelled Great Hall, where pensioners dine together at oak tables, surrounded by royal paintings; Wren's light-filled Chapel, which has a painting of the *Resurrection* above the altar by Sebastiano Ricci (1714), who clearly thought Christ was an Englishman, for he rises from the dead waving St George's flag. There is also a small museum displaying the Sovereign's Mace, presented by the Queen in 2002. The Royal Horticultural Society's Chelsea Flower Show has been held annually in the hospital grounds since 1913.

National Army Museum (14 mins)

Royal Hospital Road, SW3
Tel: (020) 7730 0717; www.national-army-museum.ac.uk
Open: daily 10am–5.30pm
Adm: free
Café, shop; Wheelchair accessible
Buses from Sloane Square 19, 21, C1

This museum tells the history of the British Army from the time of Henry VIII and the

Battle of Agincourt (1415) to the present, showing army life from the perspective of the men and women who have served in it. The permanent galleries have displays that cover five time periods, with battle reconstructions, paintings, photos and equipment. Parts of them are engagingly interactive, particularly for children: you can peer through a World War I trench telescope, test your military skills, including jungle survival, in a computer challenge; try on a Civil War helmet or lift a cannon ball. The museum's collection of authentic objects includes the skeleton of one of Napoleon's favourite horses, a section of the Berlin Wall, and the eagle standard of the French 105th regiment, which was captured at Waterloo. There are additional temporary exhibitions, lectures and special events every month for adults and children.

Chelsea Physic Garden (15 mins)

66 Royal Hospital Road
(entrance in Swan Walk), SW3
Tel: (020) 7352 5646;
www.chelseaphysicgarden.co.uk
Open: Apr–Oct Wed noon–5pm, Sun 2–6pm;
see website for special opening times in winter;
open all year to Friends of the Garden (£15)
Adm: adults £5, children £3, free to carers and
the disabled
Wheelchair accessible (call in advance)
Buses from Sloane Square 19, 21, C1

A wonderful walled garden with unusual trees, plants, herbs and seeds. Founded in 1676 by the Apothecaries' Company, it predates Kew (*see* p.178) by a century and was London's first botanical garden. It was responsible for cultivating some of England's original cedar trees in the late 17th century and in the 1730s sent the first cotton seed to the southern states of the USA to help establish the cotton industry there. Among the highlights are the world's first-ever rock garden (1772), made from stone taken from the Tower of London, and an olive tree, which once produced seven pounds of olives in a season. In the middle

Chelsea Physic Garden

is a statue of Sir Hans Sloane, physician to Queen Anne and George II, who developed the garden in the 18th century and whose collection of art and antiquities formed the nucleus of the British Museum (*see* p.37) after his death in 1753.

Carlyle's House (20 mins)

24 Cheyne Row, SW3
Tel: (020) 7352 7087; www.nationaltrust.org.uk
Open: Apr–Oct Wed–Fri 2–5pm, Sat–Sun and bank hol Mons 11am–5pm, last adm 4.30pm
Adm: adults £3.80, children £1.80; free to National Trust members
Buses from Sloane Square 19, 21

Thomas Carlyle, the 'sage of Chelsea', was the Scottish author of two best-selling historical works, *The French Revolution* and *Frederick the Great* (now all but forgotten) and the founder of The London Library in St James's Square. He moved with his wife, the tempestuous poet Jane Carlyle, to this house in 1834 and the couple became a part of literary London with Charles Dickens, William Makepeace Thackery, Alfred Tennyson and George Eliot as regular visitors. The red-brick Queen Anne house has been kept virtually intact and has been in the care of the National Trust since 1930. With its rich Victorian colours, oil lamps, original fireplaces and decoupage screens, the house conjures up a strong sense of the period, as well as providing a vivid portrait of the couple who lived beneath its roof.`

SOUTH KENSINGTON

see **Piccadilly line, p.140**

Natural History Museum p.140, Victoria & Albert Museum p.142, Brompton Oratory p.143, Science Museum see p.144, Royal Albert Hall p.146, The Fulham Road p.147

HIGH STREET KENSINGTON

It's hard to believe that Kensington was once just a country town outside London; these days it's a weathly suburb of the city, internationally famous as the former home of Diana, Princess of Wales, and for the boy who would not grow up, Peter Pan. The High Street itself is another centre for shopping, much of it consisting of major chains, but **Kensington Church Street** has some smaller and more interesting shops. walk up here and you will reach Notting Hill Gate (**see** p.52).

Kensington Gardens (5 mins)

Tel: (020) 7298 2141; www.royalparks.gov.uk
Open: daily 6am–dusk
Adm: free

Originally part of Hyde Park (**see** p.32), Kensington Gardens covers 275 acres of land and is a wonderful place to relax in central London. The main features of the park include **Kensington Palace**, the **Serpentine Gallery** and the **Albert Memorial**, **see** below. There are two playgrounds; one of these is the *Diana Playground*, situated near the Black Lion Gate (under-13s; for information tel: (020) 7298 2141), with a café (tel: (020) 7727 9578; open summer 10am–8pm, winter until 4pm). Nearby is the *Elfin Oak* (1928), an 800-year-old oak stump carved with fairies, elves and woodland creatures by children's book illustrator Ivor Innes. Sadly it is now surrounded by a fence to protect the little people from prying fingers. George Frampton's famous bronze statue of *Peter Pan* (1911), playing his pipes among squirrels, rabbits and mice, is on the east

Maggie Jones's

6 Old Court Place, W8

Tel: 0871 223 8083

Expensive

Traditional British food served in generous portions, in a cosy farmhouse atmosphere.

Wódka

12 St Alban's Grove, W8

Tel: (020) 7937 6513

Open: Mon–Fri 12.30–2.30pm, 7–11.15pm, Sat–Sun 7–11.15pm

Expensive

Modern Polish food and probably the purest vodka to be found in the capital. Moderately priced. Reservations essential.

side, next to the Long Water. His creator, J.M. Barrie, met the inspirational Llewelyn-Davies children here. At the *Round Pond* you can sail model boats, feed the ducks and sit in a deckchair (fee: Apr–Sept only). There are refreshment points in the *Italian Gardens* and by the Albert Memorial (open summer 10am–8pm, winter until 4pm).

The Orangery

Kensington Palace

Tel: (020) 7376 0239

Moderate

Open: winter daily 10am–5pm, summer daily 10am–6pm

Elegant café next to the Palace, with a terrace that is sublime in summer.

Kensington Palace (10 mins)
Kensington Gardens
***Tel**: 0870 751 5170; www.hrp.org.uk*
***Open**: Mar–Oct daily 10am–6pm; Nov–Feb daily 10am–5pm, last adm 1 hr before close;*
***Adm**: (includes audioguide) adults £10.80, children 5–16 £7, concessions £8.20, families £32; £1 off tickets bought online; joint tickets with the Tower of London or Hampton Court Orangery café, gift shop*
Wheelchair access to Royal Ceremonial Dress Collection and Orangery but not State Apartments

Monarchs William and Mary made this their home in 1689, having appointed Sir Christopher Wren to transform the Jacobean house they had bought in the village of Kensington into something with a bit more style.

 Kensington continued to be favoured as the royal residence until George III decided to move to Buckingham House. Queen Victoria was born here in 1819 and, more

Kensington Palace, Kensington Gardens

recently, it was the home of Diana, Princess of Wales (1981–1997). Diana's private apartments are not open to the public but you can visit the palace for tours of the State Apartments, including the King's Gallery, which has painted episodes of Homer's *Odyssey* on the ceiling, and the room where Queen Victoria was baptised. There is also the royal dress collection, which includes the flamboyant coronation garb of George IV and the comparatively sober costume worn by Victoria at her coronation in 1837.

Serpentine Gallery (15 mins)
Kensington Gardens, southeast side
Tel: *(020) 7402 6075;*
www.serpentinegallery.org
Open: *10am–6pm daily*
Adm: *free; Wheelchair accessible*

This small, bright pavilion was once a popular tearoom but is now transformed and mounts several first-class exhibitions of modern art every year. The shows are often a little off-the-wall but are always worth a visit, especially as it's free to get in. French windows look out onto the lake, home to countless ducks and dotted with rowing boats during the summer. An open-air café a little way along from the gallery serves non-alcoholic drinks and light snacks. The tiny birds are so tame here that they will eat out of your hand. Should you wish to stretch your legs you can walk round the lake, over the Serpentine Bridge (built in 1826 by George Rennie) and cross over into Hyde Park (***see*** p.32).

Albert Memorial (18 mins)
*Kensington Gardens; south side, opposite the Royal Albert Hall (**see** p.146); you can also get here from Knightsbridge or South Kensington*

The Albert Memorial was erected by Queen Victoria to honour her deceased husband, Prince Albert. It had been proposed before his death in 1861 but he was against the idea, saying, 'if (as is very likely) it became an artistic monstrosity, like most of our monuments, it would upset my equanimity

to be permanently ridiculed and laughed at in effigy'. One wonders what he would think of the result: designed by George Gilbert Scott and completed in 1876, Albert's gilded bronze statue can be seen gleaming from quite a distance away (and some would say this is the best way to see it).

The monument is a hotch-potch of polished and carved stone, wrought iron, gilding, bronze and mosaic. It is densely populated by allegorical figures referring to all that the Victorians esteemed – after all, Albert believed that 'public monuments should be in art the expression of our present condition and civilisation', and so there are marble groups of Asia, Europe, Africa and America, and employment of the Useful Arts (agriculture, manufacture, engineering and commerce). On the pillars are bronze statues depicting Astronomy, Chemistry, Geology and Geometry; above, in niches, are Rhetoric, Medicine, Philosophy and Physiology. The Poets frieze shows the seated Dante, Homer and Shakespeare, Goethe in the long coat and Schiller to his right, and Michelangelo gets two credits in other friezes. In the niches of the spire, if you can see them, are Faith, Hope, Charity, Humility, Fortitude, Prudence, Justice and Temperance. Albert gazes out ponderously from beneath the canopy, casually holding the catalogue from his Great Exhibition. The gilding was removed during World War II for fear of it being spotted by enemy bomber pilots, but the entire memorial has been restored in recent years.

Holland Park, *see* p.30

Holland Park, *see* p.30

Leighton House Museum (15 mins)

12 Holland Park Road, W14
Tel: *(020) 7602 3316; www.rbkc.gov.uk*
Open: *house: Wed–Mon 11am–5.30pm and spring/summer bank hols;*
Garden: Apr–Sep (weather dependent)
Guided tours: *Wed–Thu 2.30pm*
Adm: *adults £3, concessions £1, family £6*
Gift shop

In the opposite direction from Kensington Gardens (turning left out of the station and down the high street), you will find the extraordinarily exotic home of the great artist Lord Frederick Leighton (1830–96). It is a bit of a trek but worth the walk and you can window-shop along the way.

From the outside, it looks like any common-or-garden brick Victorian house. However, the interiors are impossibly breathtaking, notably the *Arab Hall* with its mosaic floor, mashrabiyya wooden screens, bubbling fountain and domed ceiling. It most celebratedly contains over a thousand priceless painted Islamic tiles collected from Syria, Egypt and Rhodes. The rest of the house is equally sumptuous: Leighton's enormous studio, where he created his wonderfully realistic and sensual Pre-Raphaelite scenes, has a massive north window; this is where he often hosted musical evenings. Paintings in the museum come from Leighton's own collection, and include works by his contemporaries such as John Everett

Leighton House

Millais, Edward Burne-Jones and George Frederick Watts. Works by Leighton himself include the skilfully lit *Death of Brunelleschi* (1852); *A Noble Lady of Venice* (1865), with marvellous detail in her clothing; and a rather butch *Clytemnestra* (*c.*1874).

Gabriel's Wharf

JUBILEE LINE

The Jubilee Line is the most recently built of London's underground tube lines. The newest part, the Jubilee Line Extension, opened in 1999 and runs eastwards from Waterloo to Stratford. This section boasts some of London's most groundbreaking engineering and architecture, which is manifest in its stations; project architect Roland Paoletti commissioned other internationally reputed architects such as Sir Norman Foster (Canary Wharf), Will Alsop (North Greenwich) and MacCormac Jamieson Prichard (Southwark and Bermondsey). The result has been compared to the rebuilding of the City churches after the Great Fire in 1666, and the simultaneous opening of so many public spaces has generated considerable excitement.

BAKER STREET

see Bakerloo line, p.14

Madame Tussaud's and the London Auditorium p.14,
Sherlock Holmes Museum p.16

BOND STREET

see Central line, p.33

Handel House Museum p.34, Selfridges p.35, The
Wallace Collection p.36

GREEN PARK

see Victoria line, p.167

Green Park p.167, The Ritz p.168, Royal Academy of Arts
p.169, Fortnum and Mason's p.170, Faraday Museum
p.170, Spencer House p.171

WESTMINSTER

Parliament Square (2 mins)

Parliament Square was created in 1868 to
allow more open space for a fitting
approach to the Houses of Parliament. It is
full of statues to notable statesmen,
including Sir Robert Peel, Benjamin Disraeli,
Abraham Lincoln and, most famous, that of
Sir Winston Churchill in hunched stance,
looking out towards Westminster Bridge.

Houses of Parliament (4 mins)

Parliament Square, SW1
Tel: (020) 7219 4272; www.parliament.uk
Open: *note that visiting is by guided tour only
(the 'Line of Route') and lasts 75 mins.
For overseas visitors: Summer Opening only; for
UK residents: Mon–Wed mornings and Fri
depending on sittings; times are subject to
change, see website or call for further details.*
Adm: *overseas visitors: adults £7, concessions
and under-16s £5, family £22; free to UK residents
Wheelchair access to most areas*

The Palace of Westminster was established
in the 11th century by Edward the Confessor
and became Parliament's official home in
1532 when Henry VIII decided to decamp to
Whitehall. Following a fire in 1834, all that
remains of this original complex are
Westminster Hall and the Jewel Tower (**see**

**The Footstool
Restaurant Gallery**

*St John's, Smith
Square, SW1*

Tel: (020) 7222 2779

*Open: Mon–Fri
11.30am–2.45pm;
plus concert
evenings (see
website or call),
Mon–Fri from
5.30pm, Sat–Sun and
hols from 6pm*

Expensive

Simple but classy
food in the brick-
vaulted crypt of St
John's church;
there's a fixed-price
menu in the
evenings (booking
recommended), and
at lunchtime a hot
or cold buffet.

The Clock Tower which houses the bell known as Big Ben

below). The present building is the work of architects Charles Barry and Augustus Pugin whose grandiose neo-Gothic masterpiece was selected from among 97 other designs submitted after the fire.

The Clock Tower is 100m (320ft) high and was not completed until 1858. It contains the 13-ton bell known as Big Ben (named either for the Commissioner of Works, Benjamin Hill, or a local pub owner, Benjamin Caunt). The distinctive throaty bong is the result of a large crack, which appeared when the bell was being installed.

To find out more, visit the Jewel Tower (at the opposite end of Parliament to Big Ben, in Abingdon Street); built in 1356 to house Edward III's jewels, it contains a special exhibition on Parliament's past and present. Westminster Hall is also included in the 'Line of Route' tour; one of Europe's largest medieval halls, this famous building dates from 1097 and is the only surviving part of the original Westminster Palace. It was originally a banqueting hall, but was later used as a venue for the Grand Council and early Parliaments, and it housed the Law Courts for 600 years. It has a spectacular 14th-century oak hammerbeam roof. In 2002, the late Queen Mother lay in state in here to allow the public to pay their respects.

It isn't easy to visit the enormous Parliament building – which has two miles of corridors, 1,100 rooms, 100 staircases, 11 courtyards and eight bars – but, if you are prepared to queue up, you can watch a debate from the Visitors' Gallery. The queue for the Lords is usually shorter, but don't expect a seat before 5pm. For a more comprehensive tour, apply to your MP or embassy at least two months in advance; details of this and all visiting procedures are posted on the website.

St Margaret's Church (3 mins)

Westminster Abbey, St Margaret Street, SW1
www.westminster-abbey.org
Open: *Mon–Fri 9.30am–3.45pm, Sat 9.30am–1.45pm, Sun 2–5pm*
Wheelchair accessible

St Margaret's Church

St Margaret's was built in the late 11th century by the monks of the Benedictine Abbey of Westminster because they were fed up of being disturbed by the locals coming to hear them at Mass. The original was demolished during Edward III's reign, and the current church was built between 1482 and 1523, although it has been restored several times since.

St Margaret's has been the parish church of the House of Commons since 1614 (all MPs are parishioners), and dotted around the interior you'll see the symbol of the Commons, a portcullis. The east window *c*.1526 commemorates Henry VIII's marriage to Catherine of Aragon and there are several other monuments and memorials to distinguished historical figures. Famous people who have been married here include Samuel Pepys in 1655, John Milton in 1656 (his second, commemorated in the window at the west end of the north aisle) and Winston Churchill in 1908. William Caxton (1491) and Sir Walter Raleigh (1618), who is commemorated in the west window, are buried here.

Westminster Abbey (5 mins)

Dean's Yard, SW1
Tel: *(020) 7654 4900*
www.westminster-abbey.org
Open: *nave, royal chapels, Statesman's Aisle and Poets' Corner: Mon–Fri 9.30am–3.45pm*

The West Front, Westminster Abbey, Dean's Yard

(Wed until 7pm), Sat 9.30am–1.45pm; chapter house: daily 10am–4pm; Museum: daily 10.30am–4pm; cloisters: daily 8am–6pm; College Garden: Apr–Sep 10am–6pm, Oct–Mar 10am–4pm
Adm: *adults £7.50, under-16s £5, families £15, under-11s free (free adm for services or prayers)*
Guided tours: *Mon–Sat (£4); tel: (020) 7654 4900 to book; Wheelchair accessible*

Westminster Abbey is the most ancient of London's great churches. it originated in the 11th century and was rebuilt in its present Gothic form in the 13th century by Henry III. It was called 'West Minster' to distinguish it from old St Paul's (**see** p.44), which was the 'East Minster' of the city. Nearly every British monarch has been crowned here and many of them, including Edward the Confessor, Henry III, Edward I, Henry VII, Elizabeth I, Charles II, William III, Anne and George II, are buried here, too. More recently, the funeral of Diana, Princess of Wales, took place here in 1997.

Its content make up the history of the nation. Among the most visited spots are memorials to the Battle of Britain (dedicated in 1947) and the *Tomb of the Unknown Warrior*, where an anonymous World War I soldier is buried, in memory of fallen soldiers from both World Wars. In *Statesman's Aisle* you can find prime ministers galore, including Palmerston, Gladstone and Disraeli while in *Poet's Corner*

The Cenotaph,
Whitehall

are dedications to literary men and women, including Geoffrey Chaucer, Samuel Johnson and Alfred Tennyson (who are buried here), William Shakespeare, Jane Austen and William Wordsworth (who are not) and Ben Jonson (who is buried upright). Sir Isaac Newton, James Watt and Michael Faraday represent the world of science and engineering. Surprisingly, there is only one painter, Godfrey Kneller, court painter to Charles II, whose dying words, 'By God, I will not be buried in Westminster Abbey', appear to have been ignored. You can see some of his work at Tate Britain (*see* p.174) and the National Portrait Gallery (*see* p.135). The Abbey's museum is worth visiting if only to see the armour worn by Henry V when he defeated the French at the Battle of Agincourt in 1415.

Whitehall (2 mins)

Opposite the Abbey on Parliament Square lies Whitehall, a name that means one thing to most ears: government. This area is mainly government offices, such as the Ministry of Defence, the Treasury and, of course, **Downing Street**, home to the Prime Minister (no.10) and the Chancellor of the Exchequer (no.11). In the middle of the road, where Whitehall becomes Parliament Street, is the **Cenotaph**, a white marble monument designed by Edward Lutyens in 1919–20, which commemorates the dead of both World Wars.

The Old Shades
37 Whitehall, SW1
Tel: (020) 7321 2801
Inexpensive
Wood panelling and floors, an open fire and old prints contribute to this Grade II-listed pub's comfort and charm.

Cabinet War Rooms (5 mins)

Clive Steps, King Charles Street, SW1
***Tel**: (020) 7930 6961; www.iwm.org.uk*
***Open**: Apr–Sep daily 9.30am–6pm, Oct–Mar
daily 10am–6pm (last adm 45 mins before close)*
***Adm**: adults £7.50, concessions £6/4/3.50,
under-16s free; includes free audioguide*
Wheelchair accessible

These cramped, claustrophobic, bombproof
rooms have remained largely unchanged
since the final years of World War II, when
they were the nerve centre for the British
war effort. The Cabinet Room looks set for
a tense meeting, pins chart the direction of
the Allied campaign in the *Map Room*, the
Telephone Room's hot line is ready for an
urgent call to the White House and, in
Winston Churchill's bedroom, a nightshirt is
laid out and a chamber pot sits under the
bed. In the *Prime Minister's office* (a former
broom cupboard) you can still see the desk
where Churchill sat when he told a war-
weary nation that this was to be their
finest hour.

A new addition to the Rooms is the
Churchill Museum, which focuses on the
life and achievements of Sir Winston
Churchill. This is organized by five themes
and periods pertaining to the great man's
life, with large-scale graphics and displays,
and an interactive timeline table that
allows visitors to explore images,
documents and film clips in detail.

Banqueting House (5 mins)

Whitehall
***Tel**: 0870 751 5178 (bookings); www.hrp.org.uk*
***Open**: Mon–Sat 10am–5pm, last adm 4.30pm*
***Adm**: adults £4, concessions £3, children £2.60,
under-5s free; includes audioguide*
Wheelchair accessible

Halfway along Whitehall, the white façade
of Banqueting House is the only remaining
building belonging to Whitehall Palace,
which was the sovereign's main residence
from 1530 to 1698, when it was destroyed
by fire. The building was designed by Inigo
Jones for King James I, with a splendid

Main Hall for court masques and state occasions. The first Renaissance structure in London, it was completed in 1622, and in 1636 James's son Charles I commissioned Peter Paul Rubens to paint the enormous and glorious ceiling panels, celebrating his father's rule and life. Charles was forced to make a poignant exit out of one of the windows onto a scaffold 13 years later, where he was beheaded before the crowds.

Horse Guards (7 mins)
Whitehall
On guard: 10am–4pm daily; Changing of the Guard: Mon-Sat 11am, Sun: 10am

A popular attraction, not least because the Queens's Life Guards never move a muscle, inspite of all the gawping and photos being taken. Household troops have guarded the royal palaces since 1660. The court was at Whitehall until 1689, when it moved to St James's Palace (*see* p.73). On the accession of Queen Victoria in 1837, it moved to its current home, Buckingham Palace (*see* p.74). To mount anew guard, the Life Guards march from Hyde Park Corner via Constitution Hill and along the Mall to Horse Guards Parade. Get here early if you want a good spot.

The Queen's Life Guard, Whitehall

WATERLOO

see **Bakerloo line, p.19**

The Queen's Walk p.19, The London Eye p.19, County Hall p.21, County Hall Gallery p.21, London Aquarium p.21, Namco Station p.21, Saatchi Gallery p.22, Dalí Exhibition p.23, IMAX Cinema p.23

SOUTHWARK

Note; Southwark's sights can also be reached via a leisurely walk along the river on The Queen's Walk (see p.19)

Tate Modern (14 mins)
Bankside
Tel: (020) 7401 5120; www.tate.org.uk
Open: Sun–Thu 10am–6pm, Fri–Sat 10am–10pm
Adm: free, charges for special exhibitions
Shops, restaurant and cafés.
Wheelchair accessible

Tate Modern, Turbine Hall

Livebait

43 The Cut, SE1

Tel: (020) 7928 7211

Expensive

Great fish restaurant (one of several in London), even though it's a little pricy.

Almost overnight, modern art became acceptable when Tate Modern opened its doors in 2000. Visit the old Tate (now Tate Britain; *see* p.174) up the river at Pimlico and it is comparatively empty – at Tate Modern you can hardly move for people. Designed by Sir Giles Gilbert Scott (who invented the English red telephone box) as a power station in 1947, the building was converted by the Swiss architects Herzog & de Meuron, who constructed a two-storey glass 'lightbeam' to flood the vast main turbine hall with natural light. Additional light comes via the illuminated bay windows on the third and fifth floors, which offer a spectacular view of the hall below.

Tate Modern displays its collection of international modern art from the 19th century to the present day thematically rather than chronologically. Artists include Dalí, Duchamp, Freud, Matisse, Picasso, Pollock, Rothko and Warhol. Umbrella topics trace links and resonances between artists who might otherwise seem to have little in common. So, for example, in Landscape/Matter/Form (3rd floor) you can find Claude Monet's 19th-century *Waterlilies* next to Richard Long's 20th-century mud paintings, to highlight both artists' similar sense of immersion in landscape. Much of the work on show, such as Marcel Duchamp's *Fountain* (actually a urinal) and Carl André's *Equivalent Viii* (a pile of bricks), questions our very notions of what art is. Peter Fischli and David Weiss, for instance, have constructed what looks like an unfinished room, waiting for paintings to be hung – you could easily walk right past. Yet every object here has been hand-carved from polyurethane foam and painted by hand. Up on the 5th floor in History/Memory/Society the Fluxus collective invite us to see everything as art except for the work found in museums. In the same room, you can try your hand at a game of Fluxipingpong using impossible bats – one bat has a large hole, another a tin can attached to it which sends the ball zipping off in every direction but the one you intended (bring your own ball).

There is far too much to see in a single day. To help get the most from your visit, audio guides can be picked up from a variety of information points (children's versions are available).

Millennium Bridge (6 mins)

Just in front of Tate Modern is the infamous steel footbridge now commonly known as the Wobbly Bridge. A collaborative effort between engineers Arup, architect Sir Norman Foster and sculptor Sir Anthony Caro, the bridge opened in June 2000 and was hailed for achieving such slightness

Millennium Bridge

while spanning such a breadth. On its first day between 80,000 and 100,000 people crossed over, but the movement of the crowds caused the structure to sway up to 7cm (3 in) from side to side – a moment captured visibly on TV news reports. The bridge was closed shortly afterwards, and tests using crowds of volunteers, including yomping army soldiers, allowed engineers to find and solve the problem; the bridge was fully reopened in early 2002. Crossing it takes you to St Paul's Cathedral and the city (*see* p.44).

Oxo Tower Wharf (12 mins)

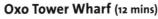

www.oxotower.co.uk
Shops open: Tue–Sun 11am–6pm
Wheelchair accessible

This Art Deco tower on the South Bank was built in 1928 on top of an old power station. Something of a landmark, the glass 'OXO' letters on the tower are part of the design – which is how the owners got away with advertising their famous stock cubes – and are lit up in red at night. In 1996 the building was rescued from dereliction and today contains flats and small shops selling artisan jewellery, glassware, home accessories, fashion and textiles. On the ground floor are commercial art galleries (the.gallery@oxo and Bargehouse) showing contemporary work, and there's a smart modern restaurant and bar on the eighth floor as well as a viewing platform.

Oxo Tower

Brasserie Bar
Oxo Tower, 8th Floor
Tel: (020) 7803 3888
Expensive
Come up here for the view. The food is good and cocktails delicious.

Gabriel's Wharf (14 mins)

www.gabrielswharf.co.uk
Shops open: *Tue–Sun 11am–6pm*

A short walk east along the river from the South Bank (*see* p.23) is Gabriel's Wharf, a homely selection of mini-shops, boutiques, restaurants and bars as well as sculpture, ceramics, fashion and jewellery workshops. It is also a nice spot to sit out. Roughly hewn hobby horses (and other animals) are free for kids to play on and there is often some form of live music on the bandstand.

LONDON BRIDGE

Attractions detailed here are to the west of London Bridge. For attractions to the east of London Bridge, **see** *p.117 (Northern Line Bank Branch).*

Once upon a time there was only one bridge that crossed the Thames. That bridge, the original London Bridge stood for centuries with houses built on it as early as 1201 (some as high as seven storeys), a chapel in the middle dedicated to Sir Thomas Becket and a drawbridge at this, the Southwark, end. It's a well-known fact that the severed heads of traitors and criminals, parboiled and dipped in tar, were put up on spikes above the gatehouse from 1305–c.1661 when the practice was abolished. William Wallace, Mel Gibson's *Braveheart,* was the first to be treated in this way. The bridge was replaced by a new five-arch structure in 1831 but this lasted a mere 140 years and was, in turn, replaced by the concrete span you see today.

Southwark Cathedral (3 mins)

Montague Close, SE1
Tel: *(020) 7367 6700;*
www.southwark.anglican.org
Cathedral open: Mon–Fri 7.30am–6pm, Sat–Sun and hols 8.30am–6pm
Visitor centre open: Mon–Sat 10am–6pm, Sun 11am–5pm
Adm: *by donation*
Regular lunchtime and evening concerts; call for details; Wheelchair accessible

This ancient cathedral's full name is the Cathedral Church of St Saviour and St Mary Overie. It is the fourth church to stand on this site and was begun around 1220 after a fire destroyed an earlier Norman Priory church of which it retains traces. It is the oldest Gothic church in London. St Mary Overie ('Overie' meaning 'over the water') parish church has seen much of history: during the Reformation it was surrendered to Henry VIII (when it became the parish church of St Saviour, Southwark); heretics

Southwark Cathedral

were tried and sentenced to death here in the reign of Mary Tudor; and during the reign of Elizabeth I the beautiful retro choir was rented by a baker, who ran his business there and kept his pigs in the church.

In the 16th century, most of London's theatres (such as the Globe and the Rose) were located in this area, and there are monuments to Edmund Shakespeare (William's youngest brother) and dramatists John Fletcher and Philip Massinger. The marvellously colourful and gilded tomb (*c.*1408) of John Gower, an early English poet and friend of Chaucer, sits in the north aisle; William Shakespeare is commemorated in a window (1954) and a reclining statue (1912) in the south aisle; there is also a memorial to Sam Wanamaker, the man responsible for the rebuilding of the Globe Theatre on the South Bank (*see* p.23). Most amusing is the memorial (*c.*1672) in the North Transept to a physician, Lionel Lockyer, who considered epitaphs 'vulgar' and instead has what can only be described as an advert for his 'well-known' pills inscribed on his monument.

Borough Market (4 mins)

8 Southwark Street, SE1;
www.boroughmarket.org.uk
Open: *Fri noon–6pm, Sat 9am–4pm*

London's oldest fruit and vegetable market, still trading in its original position, has also become London's favourite market due to the specialist organic and fine food market that sprang up alongside in 1999. It's a nice place to spend an hour or so and the food is delicious. Surrounding the market the streets hold a growing handful of shops, cafés and delis, such as Konditor & Cooke (Stoney Street, *see* right), De Gustibus (artisan breadmakers, 4 Southwark St), Neal's Yard Dairy (fine cheeses, 6 Park St) and Bedales (wine and foods, 5 Bedale St).

Bramah Tea & Coffee Museum (20 mins)

40 Southwark Street, SE1
Tel: *(020) 7403 5650;*
www.bramahmuseum.co.uk
Open: *daily 10am–6pm*
Adm: *adults £4, concessions and children £3.50, family £10*
Café, and tea and coffee shop
Wheelchair accessible

Edward Bramah, a one-time tea taster and commodity broker, set up this museum in the 1990s to show off his extraordinary collection of coffee-makers and teapots. They come in wonderful colours, shapes and sizes from fire-breathing dragons and ghouls to hedgehogs, petrol pumps and rosy-cheeked policemen. Besides the pots and other related bric-à-brac, the museum traces an engaging path through the history of tea and coffee-drinking in this country, from the arrival of the coffee bean in 1640 to the rise of coffee shops as unofficial centres for trade (Lloyd's of London began life as a coffee house) and the origins of the teabreak as a sacrosanct English ritual. There is an airy café where you can sample a good range of teas and coffees, including the museum's own blends.

The *Golden Hinde* (5 mins)

St Mary Overie Dock, Cathedral Street, SE1
Tel: *(020) 7403 0123; www.goldenhinde.co.uk*
Open: *May–Sept daily 10am–6pm, Oct–Apr daily 10am–5pm (call in advance as opening times depend on prebooked tours)*
Adm: *adults £3.50, concessions £3, children*

Fish!

Cathedral Street, Borough Market, SE1

Tel: (020) 7407 3803; www.fishdiner.co.uk

Expensive

Fresh daily fish is served here, 'posh fish 'n' chips'-style, or with modern European influences, or just how you like it. The location is great: in a modern glass-house looking out at Southwark Cathedral and the market.

Fuse Box

12 Stoney Street, Borough Market, SE1

Tel: (020) 7407 9888

Inexpensive

Southeast Asian fast food in this gourmet deli and buffet-style café.

Hobbs Pie and Mash Shop

Bedale Street, Borough Market, SE1

Inexpensive

Traditional London pie 'n' mash, jellied eels or fruit pies, to eat on the hoof.

Konditor & Cooke

10 Stoney Street, Borough Market, SE1

Tel: (020) 7407 5100

Inexpensive

Branch of this much-adored patisserie, which sells scrumptious hot pastries and mouthwatering cakes and chocolates.

Menier Chocolate Factory Restaurant

51–53 Southwark Street, SE1

Tel: (020) 7378 1712; www.menier.org.uk

Open: Mon–Fri 11am–3pm, Tues–Sat 6–11pm

Moderate

Just opposite the Bramah Tea and Coffee Museum, an arts centre restaurant serving mouthwatering, healthy Mediterranean dishes, including sandwiches and light snacks. The feel of the old chocolate factory has been comfortably retained, with cast-iron columns, exposed brickwork, and wood flooring and beams.

£2.50, family (2+3) £10
Tours: (1 hr, extra charge, book in advance);
Overnight Living History Experience: £40 per person plus £10 deposit (no children under 6)
'Pirate' gift shop

Head north to the river to find this wonderful reconstruction of Sir Francis Drake's flagship in which he became the first Englishman to circumnavigate the globe in 1580. Built in 1973, it has sailed 10,000 miles in its capacity as a floating museum but is now permanently moored in London. It is staffed by a jolly crew of knowledgeable actors in Elizabethan costime who will show you round all five decks and frighten the kids with tales of swashbuckling adventure and feats of endurance on the high seas. To get a real feel for what life might have been like on a 16th-century vessel, spend the night here on a Living History Experience, assuming the role of a crew member, carring out routine ship maintenance, eating Elizabethan food and sleeping in a cabin below decks.

The Golden Hinde

Clink Prison Museum (7 mins)

1 Clink Street, SE1
Tel: (020) 7403 0900; www.clink.co.uk
Open: Sept–mid-June daily 10am–6pm, mid-June–Aug (dates are weather dependent) daily 10am–9pm
Adm: adults £6, concessions and children £3.50, families £15

If you've ever wondered where the expression 'in the clink' (meaning to be in prison) comes from then all will soon be revealed. Housed on the site of the Bishop of Winchester's own private jail where, in the Middle Ages, the good bishop locked away anyone who dared challenge him or his various extortion rackets, the Clink's exhibition attempts to convey some of the horrors of medieval prison life on Bankside. The museum feels a little tired but it's difficult to truly portray the suffering of the poor unfortunates who were variously thrown into holes and left to rot, tied in chairs to be tortured with pincers and hot pokers, or thrown into vats of boiling oil. Amazingly, despite the barbaric treatment, prisoners were expected to pay their own way here. They even had to fork out for their own ball and chain.

Vinopolis, Bank End

Cantina Vinopolis

Vinopolis

*Tel: (020) 7940 8333;
www.menier.org.uk*

*Open: Mon–Sat
Noon–3pm, 6pm-
10.30pm, Sun
Noon–4pm*

Expensive

Atmospheric
restaurant with
award-winning food
underneath huge
Victoria arches

Wine Wharf

*Stoney Street,
Borough Market, SE1*

Tel: (020) 7940 8335

Moderate

Vinopolis's wine
bar – a short walk
away – kitted out
with country
leather sofas and
soft lighting in a
former Victorian
engineering
warehouse.
Serves good food
(including snacks)
as well as excellent
beers and wines.

Vinopolis (8 mins)

1 Bank End, SE1
Tel: *0870 241 4040; www.vinopolis.co.uk*
Open: *Mon, Fri–Sat noon–9pm, Tue–Thu, Sun
and hols noon–6pm (last adm 2 hrs before
closing)*
Adm: *adults £12.50, concessions £11.50, under-
16s free (£1 off Tue–Thu); discounts for online
booking or on tel: 0870 4444 777 (24 hrs)*
Wine bar, brasserie, refectory
Wheelchair accessible

Located in a complex of beautifully
converted brick-vaulted cellars and railway
arches, Vinopolis gives you the chance to
tour the world's wine regions on the banks
of the Thames. There are imaginative
multimedia presentations for each section –
for example, you can 'tour' the Tuscan wine
villages aboard a (stationary) Vespa. Adult
tickets include vouchers for five wine
tastings, chosen from regional tables, and
experts are on hand for occasional tutored
tastings. At the end of the tour you can visit
a wine warehouse to pick up a few select
vintages (now that you know which are the
good ones) and the wine shop to pick up
natty corkscrews, wine racks, books and
other wine-related paraphernalia. There's
also an art gallery and a wine school.

Shakespeare's Globe (12 mins)

Bear Gardens, New Globe Walk, SE1
*Shakespeare's Globe Exhibition tel: (020) 7902
1500; box office tel: (020) 7401 9919;
www.shakespeares-globe.org*

Shakespeare's Globe Theatre

Open: *Oct–Apr daily 10am–5pm, Apr–Sep 9am–noon for exhibition and guided tour of theatre, 12.30–5pm for exhibition and visit to Rose Theatre site; tours every 15–30 mins; performances: May–Sep (£5–29);*
Adm: *adults £8.50, concessions £7, under-15s £6, under-5s free, family £25*
Shop, restaurant and café
Wheelchair accessible

Many of Shakespeare's plays, including *Romeo and Juliet*, *King Lear* and *Macbeth*, were first performed on Bankside at the famous O-shaped theatre that stood a few hundred feet away from the present reconstruction. The original theatre burnt down when a spark from a stage cannon set fire to the roof during a performance of *Henry VIII*. Some 400 years later, the new Globe has been rebuilt using traditional methods and materials and is as close to the original as possible except for the addition of a few modern safety features (such as sprinklers).

The performances of the plays, too, aim to be authentic. A huge stage pokes out into an unseated area, open to the elements, with room for 500 standing (known as groundlings) who may at any time get an authentic drenching if it starts

Mar i Terra

14 Gambia Street, SE1

Tel: (020) 7928 7628

Moderate

Fresh, authentic Spanish food served on two floors and in a courtyard; perfect in summer.

to rain. For a little more comfort, seating is provided by wooden benches in three half-timbered circular galleries. The Elizabethan audiences were a rowdy lot. Mostly drunk, they were determined to enjoy the show, and would cheer for the goodies, hiss at the baddies and pitch rotten food at the stage (and each other) if they were displeased with the performance. Modern audiences should resist the temptation to launch a hamburger at Lady Macbeth, but booing, cat-calls and general merriment are still very much part of the fun.

The theatre is one part of the complex, which also includes an extensive exhibition (open all year round) on Shakespeare and his times, a fascinating look at how the Globe was rebuilt and a lively guided tour round the auditorium (also available to prebooked groups is a tour of the remains of the Rose Theatre, the first theatre to be built in Southwark in 1587; *see* www.rosetheatre.org.uk). If you visit only one theatre in London, make it this one.

Continue along the riverside walk and you will come to the South Bank (*see* pp.19-24), for sights such as the London Eye, Saatchi Gallery and the National Theatre and Southbank arts complex.

HMS Belfast

NORTHERN LINE (BANK BRANCH)

In 1890 the City and South London Railway (renamed the Northern Line in 1937) opened the world's first deep-level electric railway, which ran from the City to Stockwell. The trains could seat fewer than 100 passengers and were dimly lit by electric lights, which flickered with fluctuations in the current. Each carriage had high-backed seating and frosted windows out of which nothing could be seen, and it was not long before they became known as 'padded cells' by the people who travelled in them. At 17.25 miles, the stretch of tunnel between East Finchley and Morden is one of the longest continuous rail tunnels in the world.

NORTHERN LINE
(BANK BRANCH)

EUSTON

see **Victoria line, p.162**

St Pancras New Church p.162, British Library p.163

KING'S CROSS ST PANCRAS

King's Cross station, terminus of the Great Northern Railway, is not a pretty place.

However, in 2005 changes are in progress as an exciting development is afoot: St Pancras Station is being extended to accommodate Eurostar trains. The new Channel Tunnel Rail Link will link the station with the Channel Tunnel and provide a swifter connection between the north of Britain and the continent (it is due for completion in 2007). St Pancras Chambers, the old hotel, will be restored to hotel use, and have apartments on the upper levels.

London Canal Museum (10 mins)

12–13 New Wharf Road, N1
***Tel**: (020) 7713 0836;*
www.canalmuseum.org.uk
***Open**: Tue–Sun 10am–4.30pm (last adm 3.45pm) and bank holiday Mons*
***Adm**: adult £3, concessions £2, children £1.50 (under-8s free)*
Gift shop; Partly wheelchair accessible, but phone ahead or see website

During Britain's Industrial Revolution, canal boats brought the materials and products from the mechanized north into London to be used in the capital or sold abroad. The warehouse that houses this museum was built in the 1850s by an Italian-speaking Swiss immigrant, Carlo Gatti, who made his pile importing ice from Norway. Here you can learn about Gatti's story, peek into the huge ice wells where the ice blocks were stored, explore restored canal boats and learn about the lives led by the canal workers (adults and children) who scratched a tough living ferrying cargo in and out of the capital.

Diwana Bhel Poori House

121 Drummond Street, NW1

Tel: (020) 7387 5556

Inexpensive

Lightly spiced but hearty vegetarian food from South India, at bargain prices. The buffet is great value.

Prince Arthur

80–82 Eversholt Street, NW1

Tel: (020) 7387 2165

Moderate

Friendly and comfortable pub serving Thai food.

The King's Head

115 Upper Street, N1

Tel: (020) 7226 1916; www.kingsheadthea tre.org

Open: Mon–Thurs 11am–1am, Fri–Sat 11am–2am, Sun noon–12.30am

Inexpensive

A theatre pub with good bar food and the quaint affectation of charging for drinks using the pre-decimal system of pounds, shillings and pence. Live music is played every night after the theatre show.

Casale Franco

134–137 Upper Street, N1

Tel: (020) 7226 8994

Expensive

The long queues attest to the tastiness and good value of the spicy Italian dishes and crusty pizzas served in this lively north-London restaurant.

Fish Shop on St John Street

360–362 St John Street, N1

Tel: (020) 7359 1401

Open: Tues–Sat noon–3pm and 5.30–11pm

Expensive

Reasonably priced seafood, fresh from Billingsgate Market. Traditional fish in batter or more imaginative dishes such as tempura or deep-fried mussels, all served in smart, minimal surrounds.

Camden Passage

ANGEL

This station was named after the famous Angel coaching inn. The Angel was the nearest staging post to London on the Great North Road; from Jacobean times, rather than making the risky trip across the fields to the City at night, travellers would stay here until morning.

Crafts Council Gallery (3 mins)

44a Pentonville Road, N1
Tel*: (020) 7278 7700; www.craftscouncil.org.uk*
Open*: Tue–Sat 11am–5.45pm, Sun 2–5.45pm*
Adm*: free; Gift shop; Wheelchair accessible*

The Crafts Council is an independent body, funded by the Arts Council, that promotes high-quality contemporary craftsmanship in the UK. The gallery on the ground floor of the Georgian building shows craft exhibitions, many of which tour the country. Upstairs, 'Making It Yours' is an exhibition from the Council's own collection, representing British crafts, which changes annually. Beautiful, handmade original objects (jewellery, ceramics and textiles) are on sale in the shop.

Camden Passage (4 mins)

Camden Passage, off Islington High Street, N1
Open*: Wed and Sat 8.30am–3pm*

One of London's more genteel markets, 350 stallholders come here twice a week. You'll find everything from knick-knacks to antique dolls and Bakelite radios, glassware, paintings, costumes and rugs. It's all fairly picturesque and there are a numerous local pubs and restaurants to rest in after a hard morning's rummaging.

OLD STREET

White Cube Gallery (8mins)

48 Hoxton Square, N1
Tel*: (020) 7930 5373; www.whitecube.com*
Open*: Tue–Sat 10am–6pm*
Wheelchair accessible

This contemporary commercial art gallery is located in the extraordinarily trendy Hoxton area, in a former industrial building that has had two additional floors added. The upper area contains 'Inside the White Cube', where every year a different curator will put on 12 month-long exhibitions. The rest of the main space holds temporary shows by British and international artists; recent shows have included work by Antony Gormley, Doris Salcedo, Damien Hirst and Steven Meisel.

Columbia Road Flower Market (14 mins)

Columbia Road, E2 (between Gosset Street and the Royal Oak pub)
www.columbia-flower-market.freewebspace.com
***Open**: Sun 8am–2pm*

On Sundays the flower market heaves so arrive early or be prepared to jostle your way along. It's worth approaching from the west so you can make your way – eventually – to the best cafés. The flowers and plants are good quality and extremely cheap and, even if you don't buy any, the combined scent is enough to make you dizzy. Lining the street, the little Victorian shops sell pretty pots, perfumes, furnishings and knick-knacks, while some are welcoming cafés where you can buy a steaming coffee and a croissant to keep you going. Two of the best shops are: S. & B. Evans and Sons (7a Ezra St), potters selling original hand-thrown garden vessels from their workshop and pretty pot-filled

Bluu

1 Hoxton Square, N1
Tel: (020) 7613 2793
Open:Mon–Thur 10am–11.30pm, Fri–Sat 10am–midnight, Sun noon–10.30pm
Moderate

On the site of the famous old Blue Note club, this bar serves a range of tapas and cocktails and is a Shoreditch landmark. It gets very busy and cramped in the evening, though.

Hoxton Apprentice

16 Hoxton Square, N1
Tel: (020) 7749 2828
Open: Mon 6pm-10.30pm, Tue-Sat 12am-11pm, Dinner 6pm-10.30pm
Expensive

This restaurant in a beautiful Victorian neo-Gothic uilding offers a delicious menu by Pru Leith, including such delights as Cambodian salad of crab, prawns, pomegranate, and coconut, or organic pork and thyme sausages.

yard; and Idonia Van Der Bijl (no.122), which specializes in handmade products .

Geffrye Museum Restaurant

136 Kingsland Road, Shoreditch, E2

Tel: (020) 7739 9893

Inexpensive

A lovely, bright and airy restaurant serving homemade English snacks and teas at tables looking out over the museum gardens.

Geffrye Museum (15 mins)

136 Kingsland Road, Shoreditch, E2
Tel: *(020) 7739 9893/8543*
 www.geffrye-museum.org.uk
Open: *museum: Tue–Sat 10am–5pm, Sun noon–5pm; herb and period gardens: Apr–Oct, same times as museum; almshouse open first Sat of month, timed entry (£2, children free) at 11am, 12, 2 3 and 4pm*
Adm: *free*
Restaurant, gift shop
Special facilities for disabled visitors

Set in a row of 18th-century almshouses, this wonderful museum takes you on a journey through 400 years of English interiors, from 17th-century heavy oak furniture and panelling through to postwar utility and beyond. On the way you get a glimpse of past times and tastes: a late 17th-century Stuart room full of beautiful turned wood furniture; an elegant Georgian neoclassical interior modelled on the townhouse of a wealthy London gent; a mid-Victorian morning room with rich, dark colours and fabric, and highly decorated surfaces; an Arts & Crafts-style Edwardian drawing room, with Art Nouveau light fittings and oak fireplace; and a classy

The Geffreye Museum,

Moderne 1930s 'dining lounge' with muted tones and plain, smooth surfaces.

The almshouses show how occupants would have furnished their simple homes in the 18th and 19th centuries. A modern wing provides space to move the story along into the 21st century. There is also a delightful walled herb garden and four period garden 'rooms'.

BANK

St Stephen Walbrook (1 min)
39 Walbrook, EC4

Before you head off for the Bank of England or Guildhall, it's worth popping in here, to one of Sir Christopher Wren's post-Great Fire rebuildings (1672–9), where he rehearsed a few ideas he had for his new St Paul's Cathedral – the most obvious similarities are the cross-in-square layout and central dome. The church was badly bombed in 1940 but the font, pulpit, reredos, communion rails, sounding board and fittings are all original. Henry Moore sculpted the white marble altar (likened to a Camembert cheese). The Samaritans telephone helpline charity was founded here by rector Edward Chad Varah in 1950, and a phone presented to him by British Telecom is on display in a glass box.

Bank of England Museum (2 mins)
Threadneedle Street (entrance in Bartholomew Lane), EC2
***Tel**: (020) 7601 5545; www.bankofengland.co.uk*
***Open**: Mon–Fri 10am–5pm; **Adm**: free*
Gift shop; Wheelchair accessible (but you must ring in advance so ramps can be set up)

The museum traces the history of this venerable institution, known affectionately as 'the Old Lady of Threadneedle Street', which manages the national debt, issues banknotes, sets interest rates and keeps the country's gold locked up safe and sound. The first room is a reconstruction of the bank's Stock Office, designed by Sir John

Counting House
50 Cornhill, EC3
Tel: (020) 7283 7123
Open: Mon–Fri 11am–11pm
Inexpensive
An old banking hall that has been impressively converted to a huge pub. It now hosts a friendly crowd of city workers.

Jamaica Wine House
12 St Michael's Alley (off Cornhill), EC3
Tel: (020) 7626 9496
Open: Mon–Fri 11am–11pm
Inexpensive
Once the headquarters of a Victorian rum merchant, the interior of this low-key pub to remind you of the 21st (or even the 20th) century. Good, simple fare is on offer.

Silks & Spice

Temple Court, 11 Queen Victoria Street, EC4

Tel: (020) 7248 7878

Open: Mon–Thu 11am–11pm, Fri 11am–2am

Moderate

Small Thai-Malaysian curry house with music and dancing until 2am on Friday nights.

Simpson's Tavern

Ball Court, 38 Cornhill, EC3

Tel: (020) 7626 9985

Open: Mon–Fri 11am–11pm

Moderate

This chophouse tries to take you back to what dining was like 200 years ago, with steak and kidney pies, chops and steamed puddings

Soane (*see* p.39) in 1793, where mannequins of clerks and customers in period costume go about their daily business amid the mahogany counter tops and oak ledger rests. Other rooms elaborate on the history of the bank, its architecture, its survival during the Gordon Riots of 1780, the war years and the modern stock exchange. Interactive screens, bickering animatronic replicas of 18th-century politicians Charles James Fox and William Pitt, and the tantalizing display of solid gold bars in the 1930s' Rotunda make this a surprisingly enjoyable place to visit.

Guildhall (5 mins)
Off Gresham Street, EC2
Tel: *(020) 8472 3584*
Open: *daily 10am–5pm; occasionally closed for special events – call before you visit*
Adm: *free; Wheelchair accessible*

The Guildhall dates back to the 15th century and is the historic heart of the City of London. In the Middle Ages the guilds were hugely powerful, even lording it over the monarchy because of the huge sums of money that they generated. Today the building's role is purely ceremonial and used for the annual election of the Lord Mayor of London, as it has been for the last 800 years. Partly damaged during the Great Fire in 1666 and bomb damaged during World War II, it nevertheless remains, in essence, intact. The Old Hall is especially worth visiting to see the colourful, ornate banners of the 12 great livery companies – mercers, grocers, drapers, fishmongers, goldsmiths, skinners, merchant taylors, haberdashers, salters, ironmongers, vintners and clothworkers – which decorate the walls. Next to each banner is the coat of arms and motto of the respective company. Gog and Magog, the mythical giants who founded ancient Albion, are perched in the west gallery where they glower on all who enter.

Guildhall Art Gallery (5 mins)

Guildhall Yard (adjacent to Guildhall), EC2
Tel: (020) 7332 3700; www.cityoflondon.gov.uk
Open: Mon–Sat 10am–5pm, Sun noon–4pm (last adm 30 mins before closing)
Adm: adults £2.50, concessions £1, children free; free all day on Fri and rest of week from 3.30pm; free to City residents and workers (proof of address needed); Wheelchair accessible

Over 4,000 paintings, drawings and sculptures make up the Corporation of London's art collection, begun in the 17th century. There are 250 canvases on show at any one time. Part of the collection consists of pieces taking London and Londoners as their subject, dating from the 1600s to the present day. *The Opening of Tower Bridge*

Old Dr Butler's Head

2 Mason's Avenue (between Coleman Street & Basinghall Street), EC2

Tel: (020) 7606 3504

Open: Mon–Fri 11am–11pm

Inexpensive

This old London boozer was built in 1610 by William Butler, physician to King James I. It was burnt down in the Great Fire and subsequently rebuilt. Avoid lunchtimes if you don't like crowds

Guildhall Art Gallery

by William Lionel Wyllie (1894–5), *The Thames During the Great Frost of 1739* by Jan Griffier the Younger, and the anonymous *A Prospect of the City from the North* (*c*.1730) all offer absorbing glimpses into the past. The gallery's other *forte* is its popular Victorian and Pre-Raphaelite paintings, such as Frederick, Lord Leighton's *The Music Lesson*, Dante Gabriel Rossetti's ominous *La Ghirlandata* (1873) and Sir John Everett Millais' *The Woodman's Daughter* (1851). Also on display is the huge and famous *Defeat of the Floating Batteries at Gibraltar* by John Singleton Copley.

Clockmakers' Company Museum (7 mins)

The Clock Room, Guildhall Library, Aldermanbury, EC2
Tel: (020) 7332 1858; www.clockmakers.org
Open: Mon–Fri 9.30am–4.30pm
Adm: free; Wheelchair accessible

The Clockmakers' Company was founded by Royal Charter in 1631 and controlled the quality of the products, supervised the training of apprentice clockmakers begun in 1814. This is the oldest such collection in the world and includes 600 English and European watches, 30 clocks and 15 marine timekeepers, together with a number of rare horological portraits. Among the prize exhibits are John Harrison's 5th Marine timekeeper ('H5'), which made it possible for ships to chart their exact position while at sea; the pocket chronometer worn by George Vancouver when he took possession in 1792 of the island that now bears his name; and the watch worn by Sir Edmund Hillary during his ascent of Everest in 1953.

Simpson's Tavern

Ball Court, 38 Cornhill, EC3

Tel: (020) 7626 9985

Open: Mon–Fri 11am–11pm

Moderate

This chophouse tries to take you back to what dining was like 200 years ago, with steak and kidney pies, chops and steamed puddings.

LONDON BRIDGE

The sights listed here are to the east of London Bridge. For sights to the west **see** *Jubilee line pp.102-107.*

Old Operating Theatre and Herb Garrett (2 mins)

9a St Thomas's Street, SE1
Tel: (020) 7188 2679; www.thegarrett.org.uk
Open: daily 10.30am–5pm, closed 15 Dec–5 Jan
Adm: adults £4.25, under-16s £2.50, concessions £3.25, families £11

Surgery before antiseptics or anaesthetics was no joke, as you'll discover if you visit this museum. The tower once belonged to St Thomas's, which was founded as a hospital on this site in the 12th century. Most of the old buildings were demolished after the hospital moved to Lambeth in 1862 but the tower remained, bricked up and forgotten. Then, in 1958, it was discovered by an historian, Raymond Russell, who crawled through a hole in the belfry. Restored in 1968, it is now a fascinating if somewhat disturbing museum, which explores a period of surgery that saw patients blindfolded and gagged and held down by ropes on a wooden table with a box of sawdust underneath to catch the blood. Next door you can recover your senses in the Herb Garrett, which tells the history of herbal medicine during the same period.

The London Dungeon (4 mins)

28–34 Tooley Street, SE1
Tel: (020) 7403 7221; www.thedungeons.com
Open: Nov–Feb 10am–5pm daily, Mar–Oct 10am–5.30pm daily; open 9.30am–5.30pm during half term
Adm: adults £13.95, children (5–15) £9.95, concessions £7.95–11.25
Wheelchair accessible Note: the museum is not suitable for very young children or for anyone of a nervous disposition

An orgy of gore, if ever there was one. Some of the displays are a little creaky but the London Dungeon continues to pack in the crowds so it must be doing something right. Basically, if it's horrid, it's here: dark and dingy arches resound with piteous screams and wails as waxwork figures are subjected to unspeakable torture on the rack; Anne Boleyn delivers her speech on

The George Inn

George Inn Yard, 77 Borough High Street, SE1

Tel: (020) 7407 2056; www.nationaltrust.org.uk

Moderate

One of London's oldest pubs and its only remaining galleried coaching inn, with a labyrinth of interconnecting bars and a courtyard. Bar food and an à la carte restaurant (open Mon–Sat evenings).

Fina Estampa

150 Tooley Street, SE1

Tel: (020) 7403 1342

Open: Mon–Fri noon–2.30pm, 6.30–10.30pm, Sat and Sun 6.30–10.30pm

Moderate

A Peruvian restaurant, strangely situated in the heart of Ye Olde London.

the block (1536) before being decapitated; a human is sacrificed by druids at Stonehenge, and Boudicca hacks a Roman foot soldier to death. Another exhibit is devoted to the Great Fire of London, but the best part is 'Jack the Ripper': visitors are taken back in time to foggy Victorian London, where costumed actors take you through the East End on a search for the infamous murderer.

Winston Churchill's Britain at War Experience (6 mins)
64–66 Tooley Street, SE1
Tel: *(020) 7403 3171; www.britainatwar.co.uk*
Open: *Apr–Sep daily 10am–5.30pm, Oct–Mar daily 10am–4.30pm*
Adm: *adult £8.50, children 5–15 £4.50, concessions £5.50, family £18*
Wheelchair accessible

This isn't a patch on the Imperial War Museum (**see** p.26) or the Cabinet War Rooms (**see** p.95) but it's still worth a visit, especially for children. Here, to a backdrop of archive footage, radio broadcasts and the rousing tunes of Vera Lynn, you can find out a little of what life was like during World War II. Seek shelter in an Underground station during an air raid or pick your way through a darkened bomb site (with sirens wailing and spotlights searching the sky). There is a good collection of memorabilia (books, clothes, newspapers) and children are encouraged to get involved, trying on period clothes and gas masks to give them a greater sense of life in London during the Blitz.

Winston Churchill's
Britain at War Experience

HMS *Belfast*

HMS *Belfast* (9 mins)
Morgan's Lane, off Tooley Street, SE1
Tel: *(020) 7940 6300*
http://hmsbelfast.iwm.org.uk
Open: *Mar–Oct daily 10am–6pm*
(last entry 5.15pm), Nov–Feb 10am–5pm
daily (last entry 4.15pm)
Adm: *adults £7, under-16s free, concessions £5*
Limited access for wheelchair users

This 11,500-ton, 200m (656ft) battleship
was one of the most powerful cruisers the
Royal Navy ever built and was an integral
part of the fleet from 1938 until the end of
the Korean war in 1953. In that time it saw
service during the D-Day landings and the
decisive 1944 invasion of Normandy. Since
1971 it has been moored here and has
become a spectacular floating museum. It
isn't to everyone's taste but war buffs and
children will enjoy exploring the seven decks,
which include the boiler and engine rooms,
mess halls, punishment cells, operation rooms
and the massive gun turrets. As an offshoot
of the Imperial War Museum (*see* p.26), the
ship is also used to explore the history of
the Royal Navy from 1914 to the present day.

Fashion and Textile Museum
(13 mins)
83 Bermondsey Street, SE1
Tel: *(020) 7403 0222; www.ftmlondon.org*
Open: *Tue–Sun 10am–4.45pm*
(last adm 4.15pm)
Adm: *adults £6, concessions £4, families £16*
Gift shop; Wheelchair accessible

No, this outrageous orange and neon pink building hasn't landed from space, it's a museum dedicated to contemporary fashion and textile design, founded by Zandra Rhodes and designed by Mexican architect Ricardo Legoffeta – one only of 57 people to receive the Gold Medal Award from the American Institute of Architects in 93 years.

The international fashion designer-icon, renowned for her artistic, eccentric style (as well as her fuschia pink hair), created the Fashion and Textile Museum to provide a unique resource for public and students alike, showing a permanent collection of fashion from the 1950s to the present day. One of her aims is to show the artistic and technical skills involved in fashion creation, and the permanent collection comprises many of her own pieces as well as those of international big-name designers. With an eye to the future, the museum is also committed to education: as well as the main exhibition area, there is accommodation for Rhodes's student-apprentices, teaching facilities, a library and a digital archive of textile design references.

The Fashion and Textile Museum

Bermondsey (17 mins)

Bermondsey used to be known as the 'Larder of London': many food processing companies had their premises here because it was close to the docks. It was also famous for its leather market, located off Weston Street (now contains the London Glassblowing Workshop, www.londonglassblowing.co.uk) and reflected in the street names; today, many of the old warehouses in the area house restaurants, galleries and studios. The area in which the antiques market is situated is a conservation area and there are some very old buildings along Bermondsey Street itself.

Bermondsey Antique Market (17 mins)

Bermondsey Square, Long Lane and Bermondsey Street, SE1
Open: *Fridays 5am–2pm, but some stalls may close at noon*

Bermondsey Antiques Market is London's largest and most important antiques market, where over 500 traders set up stall in the square or in the covered warehouses. The place is under full steam by 6am – this is the place to come if you're looking for antiques of any sort or shape at competitive prices.

Butler's Wharf (18 mins)

Warehouses dating from 1873 are just east of Tower Bridge (**see** p.59), once the largest complex on the Thames. After redevelopment in the 1980s they became known for Sir Terence Conran's seafood restaurant Le Pont de la Tour restaurant. Since then many other restaurants have thrived in the area, which sits around a central piazza. Walking along Shad Thames (a corruption of 'St John at Thames', referring to the Knights Templar who once controlled this area), between the high structures with their hanging gantries overhead, you can imagine how gloomy and dangerous this area must have once been. To get some idea, bear in mind that in Charles Dickens' novel *Oliver Twist*, Bill

Delfina Studio Café

50 Bermondsey Street

Tel: (020) 7537 0244; www.delfina.org.uk

Open for food: Mon–Fri noon–3pm, Fri also 7–10pm

Moderate

A large, bright café in a gallery serving international cuisine from spaghetti to kangaroo. Booking advised for dinner.

Le Pont de la Tour

Butlers Wharf Building, 36d Shad Thames, SE1

Tel: (020) 7403 8403; www.conran-restaurants.co.uk

Expensive

In a civilized waterside setting, Terence Conran's successful restaurant is where you can sample marvellously succulent French-style seafood. Look out for the 'crustacea altar', displaying oysters, langoustines, clams, crab and mussels etc. in the (less expensive) bar-grill. There's also a food shop next door.

Butler's Wharf

Sykes meets his end around the old dock inlet just beyond the Design Museum: 'where the buildings on the banks are dirtiest and the vessels on the river blackest with the dust of colliers and the smoke of close-built low-roofed houses... the filthiest, the strangest, the most extraordinary of the many localities that are hidden in London'.

Design Museum Café

Tel: (020) 7940 8785

Open: daily 10am–5pm

Inexpensive

Good cakes and pastries and funky china. You don't need to visit the museum to visit the café.

Design Museum (21 mins)

Shad Thames, SE1
Tel: *0870 833 9955; www.designmuseum.org*
Open: *daily 10am–5.45pm (last adm 5.15pm)*
Adm: *adults £6, concessions £4, family £16*
Café, gift shop
Wheelchair accessible

It's not often you can walk round a museum and recognise exhibits behind the glass that you may have once owned, and perhaps still do. The brainchild of style guru Sir Terence Conran, the Design Museum presents everyday items such as radios and televisions, washing machines, cameras and vacuum-cleaners as objects to be studied and valued. Not all could be described as classics but, when set side by side, you begin to look at each in a new way and perhaps start to appreciate how revolutionary such mundane items as, say, the anglepoise lamp, truly are. The first floor of the museum is set apart for state-of-the-art design (just how small can a camera get?) as well as housing a temporary exhibition space where you might see anything from 1930s British furniture to an exhibition dedicated to video arcade games. Kids receive a free action pack, including trails, games and exercises to encourage them to learn from their visit. At the shop you can pick up your very own design classic (a period phone or a Dyson vacuum perhaps?).

Trafalgar Square

NORTHERN LINE
(CHARING CROSS BRANCH)

The Northern Line is an amalgam of what were once two separate lines: the City and South London Railway (C&SLR) and the Hampstead Tube. The C&SLR opened in 1890 and was the first electric underground railway in the world, running from King William Street in the City (between Bank and Monument stations) to Stockwell. The Hampstead Tube opened in 1907, running from Charing Cross to Golders Green, with a branch from Camden to Highgate. Under Holly Bush Hill, north of Hampstead station (the deepest on the tube network), lies the deepest tunnel in the entire London Underground system, 67.4m (221ft) below street

EUSTON

see Victoria line, p.162
St Pancras' New Church p.162, British Library p.163

GOODGE STREET

Goodge Street Shopping

Goodge Street is the only tube stop on the West End branch of the Northern Line not covered by other lines in this guide. It offers some good shopping, especially the flagship branch of **Habitat** (196 Tottenham Court Rd), for affordable modern home furnishings and a small café and **Heal's** (same address), one of London's oldest furnishing stores, which is more expensive but has the edge on style and quality.

The success of Habitat and Heal's has meant that this area of **Tottenham Court Road** has many similar shops. Further down the road is Lombok (no.108 and no.204–208), selling simple, Eastern-influenced hand-made furniture from natural or recycled materials; The Pier (no.200) is a kind of high-street equivalent; Paperchase (nos. 213–15) sells unusual and original stationery, with a coffee shop upstairs where you can look down on the street; and Purves & Purves (no.222) takes modern design to wild extremes, doing particularly creative things with plastic. Tottenham Court Road is also well known for shops selling electrical goods like hi-fi and computers. It's worth shopping around to find the best price.

Bertorelli's

19–23 Charlotte St, W1

Tel: 0871 223 8064

Moderate

Chic café and upstairs restaurant from the famous Italian chef.

Planet Organic

22 Torrington Place, WC1

Tel: (020) 7436 1929

Cheap

Delicious organic juices and wholesome takeaway lunches.

TOTTENHAM COURT ROAD

see Central line, p.37
British Museum p.37

LEICESTER SQUARE

The lights and the glitter – Leicester Square is commonly known for cinema premières and the razzle-dazzle of its nightlife. It's the heart of the West End, where London shimmies in your face and flicks you a peanut; where buskers play pan pipes or Shadows' songs, boys and girls dressed up to the nines stumble about on a night 'up west', and the big lights of the cinemas, nightclubs, restaurants and fast-food joints beckon. Leicester Square gets crowded, leery and there are pickpockets, yes; but it's great fun to feel the oomph of the throng.

As to its history, the square was laid out in the 1670s in front of the Earl of Leicester's house on the north side. The houses around the other sides fast became fashionable, and by the 18th century many aristocratic families lived here, as well as several artists: William Hogarth lived at no.30 in 1733–64 and Joshua Reynolds was at no.47 from 1760 until his death in 1792. By the late 19th century the spirit of the square had changed from a private residential area to one reputed for its Turkish baths, oyster rooms and theatres. At the square's garden gates are busts of past residents Hogarth, Reynolds, surgeon John Hunter and Isaac Newton (who in fact lived in St Martin's Street), and in the centre is a marble fountain with a figure of Shakespeare on the top.

Charing Cross Road (1 min)

Famous for its shops selling musical instruments but, even more so, for its bookshops, Charing Cross Road skirts the edge of Leicester Square, Covent Garden and Chinatown, silently threading its way through the West End. The bookshops that are best known or largest include Zwemmer (specializing in the arts and architecture; nos. 72 and 80), Blackwells (no.100), Foyle's (nos. 113–19) and Borders (no.122).

Bookshop on
Charing Cross Road

The Photographer's
Gallery

Photographers' Gallery (1 min)

5 and 8 Great Newport Street, WC2
Tel: *(020) 7831 1772; www.photonet.org.uk*
Open: *Mon–Sat 11am–6pm, Thu until 8pm, Sun
noon–6pm*
Adm: *free; Partly wheelchair accessible*

This is is the country's foremost venue for
exhibitions of contemporary photography
just off Charing Cross Road, towards Covent
Garden. There is a main exhibition area, a
specialist print- and bookshop, and a café.
The gallery shows a number of temporary
exhibitions each year and also has an
integrated programme of talks and events.

Chinatown (3 mins)

*Mainly centred around Gerrard Street
and Lisle Street, WC2*

In the 1950s, the area round Gerrard Street
and Lisle Street was fairly run down and,
attracted by the cheap rents, many Chinese
people from Hong Kong made it their
home. Now known as Chinatown, there are
a handful of Chinese supermarkets and
herbalists and a multitude of restaurants –
it's a great place to sample the delights of
Chinese cookery and to watch the world go
by. The best time to visit is during the noisy
Chinese New Year Festival (end of Jan),

**Photographer's
Gallery**

*Open Mon-Sat,
11am-6pm, Thu
11am-7.30pm, Sun
noon-6pm*

Inexpensive

Friendly attractive
café offering light
refreshments and
tea and cakes.

Fung Shing

15 Lisle Street, WC2

Tel: (020) 7437 1539

Expensive

Recently
refurbished, one of
Chinatown's best-
known restaurants
is now looking
better than ever. A
little pricy, but
worth it.

Window display, Chinatown

Harbour City

46 Gerrard Street, W1

Tel: (020) 7439 7859

Moderate

Classic steamed dim sum (Chinese dumplings) and delicious house specialities from this superior Cantonese diner. Reasonably priced.

Kettner's

29 Romilly Street, W1

Tel: 0871 223 8103

Moderate

Established in the 1860s this restaurant's best feature is the elegant Champagne Bar, where you can sit back in an armchair and enjoy a lingering glass of bubbly. The menu is an upmarket and better version of Pizza Express.

when the area is brightly decorated with paper lanterns. Stalls sell Chinese crafts and food and a parade of dancing dragons, accompanied by firecrackers and music, slithers down the street.

Soho (5 mins)

Soho can roughly be measured as the area bounded by Oxford Street to the north, Shaftesbury Avenue to the south, Charing Cross Road to the east and the Carnaby Street area to the west. Its main streets are five north–south streets: Berwick Street (*see* below), Wardour Street, Dean Street, Frith Street and Greek Street, with Old Compton Street (traditionally London's centre for gay culture) running east–west across them. Here and there, particularly around the Windmill Street area, you'll find the doorway solicitation and striptease-joint culture, for which Soho became well known in the 1960s, still lingering.

Many, many moons ago Soho was royal parkland, and set aside for hunting ('So-ho!' the hunters would cry as they rushed off in pursuit of their quarry). In the 18th century many French Huguenots and other dispossessed foreigners settled in the area, and the aristocrats who had populated the grand houses in the aforementioned streets departed. Gradually the population increased and Soho declined. By the late 19th century it had become a squalid place, full of cholera and prostitutes – but it was also a place for theatre and entertainment, and by the early 20th century, it was known for its restaurants. (The oldest and most-loved of these is Kettners, on Romilly Street, which was set up in the 1860s by a former chef to Napoleon III, and was a favourite of Oscar Wilde.) Today there are hundreds of restaurants and bars all jostling for business in Soho, where you can select from a vast choice of types of cooking.

Berwick Street Market (6 mins)
Berwick Street, W1
Open: *Mon–Sat 8am–6pm*

Londoners were first introduced to the delights of the pineapple here in 1890 and the market is still one of the best places to come for fruit and veg. Most is fairly cheap and, since it often teeters on the edge of being over-ripe, is perfect to eat the same day. The stallholders are part of the fun, clamouring for your custom and barking out ribald innuendo about their produce. On both sides of the market are several old-fashioned fabric shops (good for exotica and zebra print), a couple of greasy-spoon cafés, trendy salons and a clutch of cheap and second-hand CD and record shops.

Ed's Easy Diner
12 Moor St, W1
Tel: (020) 7439 1955
Inexpensive

Great fun, this 1950s diner serves burgers, shakes and fries as you perch on high stools listening to the juke box.

Beatroot
92 Berwick Street, London, W1
Tel: (020) 7437 8591
Inexpensive

Good, fast-food vegetarian café, offering hot food and salads. Several vegan dishes.

Bar Du Marche
19 Berwick St, W1
Tel: 0871 075 8642
Inexpensive

Ice-cold beers, good wine, and reasonably priced, well-cooked French and vegetarian food.

Berwick Street Market

Eleanor's Cross, Charing Cross station forecourt

Exotica

7 Villiers St, WC2

Tel: (020) 7930 6133

Inexpensive

Great-value, healthy fusion food, including Thai, Moroccan and Mexican dishes.

CHARING CROSS

Charing Cross was the last of 12 resting places for the funeral *cortège* of Eleanor, beloved wife of Edward I, as it travelled from Lincolnshire to Westminster Abbey in 1290. At each stop, a cross was erected. The original cross was taken down in 1647; the cross you see is a reproduction from 1863.

'Charing' is a corruption of the Old English *cierran,* meaning 'to turn' for it was here that the road from the west used to turn northwest at the river bank. In the 18th century, Charing Cross was the centre of London life; proclamations were read out and Dr Johnson (**see** p.42) once said that here you could find 'the full tide of human existence'. An Italian puppeteer is said to have given the first Punch and Judy show in England on this spot. the station was built in 1864 and was London's gateway to the continent as 'boat trains' ran from here to Folkestone, Dover and Ramsgate.

Trafalgar Square (2 mins)

Trafalgar Square is the centre of London, from which the distances of all points outside the capital are measured (there is a plaque indicating the precise place at the corner of Strand and Charing Cross Road). Begun some 170 years ago, it was laid on the site of the king's mews (all the king's horses were once lodged here). Architect John Nash,

One of Landseer's bronze lions, Nelson's Column, Trafalgar Square

drew up the original plans to create a huge open space to glorify the country's naval power, but he fell from grace before his scheme could come to fruition (*see* p.74).

The recent pedestrianization of the north side, just in front of the National Gallery, makes it more user-friendly – and the natural incline (from north to south) allows a view down Whitehall, leading to Westminster, the Mall, leading to Buckingham Palace,and Northumberland Ave, which goes down to the Thames. It is now most famous for **Nelson's Column**, commemorating Britain's most famous sailor, who lost his life beating the combined Franco–Prussian fleet in 1805, and Edwin Landseer's enormous bronze lions.

It is well-known for public gatherings, especially at Christmas and New Year, when a huge tree set up in the square, donated annually by the Norwegian people in thanks for Britain's help during the World War II.

St Martin-in-the-Fields (2 mins)

Trafalgar Square, WC2
Tel: *(020) 7766 1100*
www.stmartin-in-the-fields.org
Open: *8am–6.30pm daily*
Adm: *free; Café and gift shop*

As the heavy traffic grinds past, it is hard to imagine that this used to be 'in the fields'. Though a church has stood here since the

Café in the Crypt

Beneath St Martin-in-the-fields, Duncannon St, WC2

Tel: (020) 7839 4342

Inexpensive

Atmospheric café serving home-cooked snacks, though these days it's better for cakes and scones at teatime.

St Martin-in-the-Fields

13th century, the present building dates from 1726. Designed by James Gibbs, it is the oldest building in the square. Inside, richly ornate woodwork and plaster remind one that this is the Queen's parish church (a royal box stands to the left of the gallery). Lunchtime and evening recitals keep the visitor numbers up; in the crypt are the London Brass Rubbing Centre and a busy, atmospheric café.

National Gallery (4 mins)

Trafalgar Square, WC2
Tel: *(020) 7747 2885;*
www.nationalgallery.org.uk
Open: *daily 10am–6pm, Wed until 9pm*
Adm: *by donation*
Guided tours: twice daily (three times on Wed)
Café and restaurant, three gift shops
Wheelchair accessible

The National Gallery's collection began in 1824 when the government paid £57,000 to buy 38 pictures from a recently deceased merchant, John Julius Angerstein. Included in this original scoop was work by Raphael, Rembrandt and Van Dyck. In the Victorian era, as England grew rich on the proceeds

Crivelli's Garden Restaurant

National Gallery Level 1

Tel: (020) 774 72869

Open: 10am-5.45pm, Weds 10am-8.30pm (last food orders 7.45pm)

Inexpensive

Breakfast, lunch and supper – light bites to *à la carte* with a wonderful view over Trafalgar Square. There is also a stylish café on level 0 of the main building.

of the Industrial Revolution, the gallery engaged in numerous buying sprees. Even today it has some £2 million a year to spend. The results are staggering, with examples of virtually every major school of Western European art from the 13th to the early 20th centuries.

The oldest work (from 1260 to 1510) is kept in the new *Sainsbury Wing*, as is the excellent shop and one of two Micro Galleries where you can explore the museum's collection without budging an inch, and print out your own tour. You can also pick up a useful CD gallery guide at the top of the stairs to talk you round. Most people head for Rooms 51, 56 and 60 in the Sainsbury Wing to take in, respectively, work by Leonardo da Vinci, Van Eyck and Raphael.

You can't hope to appreciate the whole gallery in a day so make good use of the guide to help you decide where to go. The *West Wing* (1510–1600) has only 10 rooms, with Tintorettos and Titians in Room 7. In the North Wing (1600–1700) you will find the dreamy harbour scenes of Lorraine (contrasted with two works by Turner in Room 15), the quiet calm of the Dutch interiors, especially the Vermeers, in Room 16 and Samuel van Hoogstraat's ingenious peepshow in Room 17. Rembrandt's highly detailed and expressive self-portraits (Room 23) and Ruben's exuberant biblical

Entrance hall to National Gallery

scenes (Room 29), as well as the characterful portraits of Velazquez (Room 30), are also not to be missed.

The museum may seem quiet but wait until you reach the *East Wing* (1700–1900), and Rooms 43–45 in particular, which contain work by the Impressionists and Post-Impressionists, including Renoir, Monet, Van Gogh, Seurat and Cezanne. Famous paintings include Van Gogh's *Sunflowers*, Seurat's *Bathers at Asnières* and Monet's *Water Lilies*. For a little more peace, head for Room 34 to squint at Turner's *Rain, Steam and Speed* and Room 38 for the opulent barge and street scenes of Canaletto, and then to return to see the Impressionists when the museum has emptied out. (The quietest times to visit are early weekday mornings and on Wednesdays, from 6pm–9pm.)

Portrait Restaurant

National Portrait Gallery 3rd Floor Ondaatje Wing

Tel: (020) 7312 2496

Open: Sat-Wed 11.45am-2.45pm, Thu-Fri 11.45am-2.45pm (last orders), 5.30pm-8.30pm (last orders)

Expensive

An a la carte menu with British dishes

Lounge and Bar

Sat-Wed 10am-5pm, Thu-Fri 10am-8.30pm (last orders – food) 10pm (last orders drinks)

Inexpensive

New restaurant and bar overlooking Trafalgar Square and beyond. The food is good, the head chef has a Michelin star and the panoramic view is great. Book ahead at restaurant. The bard and lounge are small but perfect for a light lunch.

National Portrait Gallery (5 mins)

2 St Martin's Place, WC2
Tel: (020) 7306 0055; www.npg.org.uk
Open: Mon–Sat 10am–6pm, Sun noon–6pm
Adm: free; Wheelchair accessible

In 1856, when the NPG was founded to celebrate Britain's heroes, you had to be royalty or high in government to have your likeness hung on the walls. Today you need only be a celebrity – a poet, a pop star, a journalist, a footballer or even a cook. The sitter rather than the art is the point and, consequently, not everything is first rate. But it hardly matters as you trace English history through the faces of its movers and shakers.

The collection begins in the spruce new *Ondaatje Wing*, with the Tudors. Holbein's vivid sketch of Henry VII and Henry VIII, the amazingly clear portrait of Richard III (artist unknown) and a clever picture of Edward VI by William Scrots, which you need to view from an acute angle to see it in true perspective, are all worth seeing. Also of note is the only known portrait of Shakespeare, which is in the miniatures gallery. The current royals are now on the first floor (Room 33). Look out, too, for Bryan Organ's

youthful representation of Diana, Princess of Wales, painted before the cracks began to appear in her marriage (Room 36).

The new Balcony Gallery leads you into the 20th century and includes photos of The Beatles, George Best and Julie Christie. On the first floor, where the bulk of 20th-century portraits are, you might also bump into TV chef Delia Smith surrounded by pans, Bobby Charlton, or a shapely Darcey Bussell, gracefully dancing on points. For David Beckham fans who want to get even closer, Sam Taylor-Wood's video portrait of David Beckham sleeping – which runs for 1hr 7mins on a continuous loop – is not to be missed; it is in Room 41A.

Institute of Contemporary Arts (7 mins)

The Mall, SW1
Tel: *(020) 7930 3647; www.ica.org.uk*
Open: *Mon noon–10.30pm, Tue–Sat noon–1am, Sun noon–11pm; gallery: daily noon–7.30pm*
Adm: *Non-members: Mon–Fri £1.50, Sat–Sun £2.50; Wheelchair accessible*

Walking through the grand Admiralty Arch (1910), you come on the ash-tree-lined Mall with Buckingham Palace (*see* p.74) at its far end and St James's Park (*see* p.73) on your left. On your right is the Institute of Contemporary Arts (ICA), which opened in 1948 as a challenge to the conservatism of the major

ICA Bar and Café

Tel: (020) 7930 8619
Open: Mon: Noon-11pm
Tue-Sat noon-1am, Sun noon-10.30pm
Inexpensive

Nice and friendly, attractive space, very reasonable food (served canteen-style). Note: You need day membership or a ticket to an event to get in.

galleries. Arch modernists Henry Moore and Pablo Picasso were first exhibited in London here, as was Damien Hirst (he of the embalmed floating animals in the Saatchi Gallery, *see* p.22). Plenty of avant-garde dance and the odd film screening are also reasons to visit, as is the trendy bar-cum-café, which has chef Allegra McEvedy at the helm. It's a good place for celebrity spotting, too!

Mall Galleries (10 mins)

The Mall, SW1
Tel: *(020) 7930 6844; www.mallgalleries.org.uk*
Open: *daily 10am–5pm*
Adm: *£2.50 (concessions £1)*
Wheelchair accessible by chairlift

Further along from the ICA is Carlton House Terrace, a procession of cream-coloured John Nash terraces (1832) that count Gladstone, Lord Palmerston and Earl Grey among their former occupants. The Mall Galleries, below one of these, was opened in 1971 and is home to the Federation of British Artists, an umbrella arts organisation supporting such groups as the Royal Society of Portrait Painters and the Society of Wildlife Artists. The galleries show work by established contemporary artists as well as those who are new or unknown; here you might see anything from a graduate show to an exhibition of designer crafts. The bonus at this gallery is that if you like something you see you'll probably be able to buy it.

EMBANKMENT

see Circle line, p.71

Golden Jubilee Bridge p.71, Victoria Embankment Gardens p.71, Cleopatra's Needle p.72

WATERLOO

see Bakerloo line, p.19

The Queen's Walk p.19, The London Eye p.19, County Hall p.21, County Hall Gallery p.21, London Aquarium p.21, Namco Station p.21, Saatchi Gallery p.22, Dalí Universe Exhibition p.23, IMAX Cinema p.23, South Bank Centre p.23

Piccadilly Circus

PICCADILLY LINE

The Piccadilly Line was opened in 1906 by the Great Northern, Piccadilly and Brompton Railway. It cuts a diagonal route through London from Cockfosters in the north to Heathrow Airport in the west and serves some of London's most fashionable districts on its way. Its name is derived from 'Piccadilly Hall', a derisory nickname given to a house built in the early 1600s near Great Windmill Street belonging to a retired tailor, Robert Baker, who had made his fortune selling 'picadills' – a kind of stiff collar – to trendsetting 17th-century Londoners.

SOUTH KENSINGTON

Natural History Museum (8 mins)

Cromwell Road, SW7
Tel: (020) 7942 5000/5011; www.nhm.ac.uk
Open: Mon–Sat 10am–5.50pm, Sun 11am–5.50pm
Adm: free, charges for special exhibitions Wheelchair access via Earth Galleries entrance; most galleries wheelchair accessible

This museum was opened in 1881 after it became evident that the British Museum was too small to contain the nation's ever-expanding collection of natural history specimens. Today, with a staggering 68 million plants, animals, fossils, rocks and minerals, it is bursting at the seams. Although many of the exhibits are aimed mostly at children, few visitors will leave without a sense of awe at the complexity of our planet. Ask at the Information desk about children's activities.

The museum is split into Life Galleries and Earth Galleries, plus the new Darwin Centre. The *Life Galleries* contain what is probably the most popular exhibit – the dinosaurs. The first dinosaur you encounter, a huge 45-m (150-ft) skeleton of a plant-eating diplodocus, is in the main hall. This huge room contains some of the museum's treasures, including the skeleton of a tiny humanoid ape brought to England in 1698, a 225-million-year-old tree trunk and an egg laid by the extinct Madagascan elephant bird, which is 200 times the size of a chicken's egg. There is also a display with a scary, 'super-sensing', robotic tyrannosaurus rex. The mammals begin in Room 23. Here you encounter animals of every description. Some, like the stuffed 12cm-long pink armadillo are real. Others, such as the massive blue whale, which dominates Room 24, are fake. There is much to see, but try to make time for the hands-on Human Biology section (Room 22); the imaginative and newly updated Ecology Gallery (Room 32), which looks at current threats to biodiversity and conservation; and Creepy

Natural History Museum

The museum offers a variety of eating options.

Waterhouse Café

Open: 10am-5pm

inexpensive

For hot and cold dishes, sanwiches and cakes.

Life Galleries Restaurant

Open: 10am-5pm

Moderate

Offering three hot courses as well as snacks and childrens' menu and heating facilities for baby food.

Globe Fast-Food

Open: 11am-4pm

Inexpensive

For soups, jacket potatoes, salads, and ice cream and a snack bar and picnic area which is open 11am-4.30pm where youi can eat your own picnic. High chairs are available in all restaurants.

The Main Hall, Natural History Museum,

Crawlies (Room 33), where you can find out how many bugs share your home.

You enter the *Earth Galleries* through a stunning vaulted glass entrance with a central escalator that takes you up through the earth's inner core to 'The Power Within', where you can stand in a Japanese supermarket as it gets shaken by a massive earthquake. In 'Restless Surface' you learn what makes the winds blow and the tides turn, while 'From the Beginning' examines how life began and ends by asking some chilling questions about the planet's future. The final must-see is 'Earth's Treasury' (Room 64) – a display of precious stones. Look out for Alexandrite – a rare gem that changes colour according to whether it is under natural or artificial light.

The *Darwin Centre* is a new building that provides storage, visitor access, and laboratories for scientific research. Phase One is now open and you can see specimens close up, take guided tours and see live events hosted by scientists, curators and researchers – such as 'Flesh-eating Beetles of the Museum', explaining how the museum's skeletons are stripped. Phase Two will open in 2008 and will allow even more access plus accommodation for other research departments.

Victoria & Albert Museum (9 mins)

Cromwell Road, SW7
Tel: *(020) 7942 2000; www.vam.ac.uk*
Open: *daily 10am–5.45pm; Wed and last Fri of month until 10pm*
Adm: *free, charges for special exhibitions*
Phone or check website for talks, events and children's activities
3 gift shops, 2 cafés; Wheelchair accessible (use Exhibition Road entrance or call **Tel**: *(020) 7938 8638 to book an escort in advance)*

This huge, sprawling, pick-'n'-mix of a museum, once defined by a former director as an 'extremely capacious handbag', never fails to satisfy whether you are visiting for the first or the hundredth time.

Originally intended as the permanent version of the 1851 Great Exhibition, the V&A is now a vast and eclectic collection of the Decorative Arts. There are seven miles of corridors and 145 galleries housing art, and design and sculpture from around the world: armour, silverware, tapestries (including seven huge tapestry cartoons by Raphael), musical instruments, plaster casts, wrought-iron work, furniture, clothes, textiles, household items, posters, photographs, toys, household appliances....

Some of the highlights are worth seeking out before you are completely exhausted. The *Plaster Cast Hall* (Level 1, Rooms 46a–b) has re-creations of some of the world's most famous (and biggest) sculptures, including Michelangelo's *David* (plus his separately displayed fig leaf) and *Moses* and the colossal *Trajan's Column* from Rome. The *20th-century Gallery* (Level 3, Rooms 70–74 and 103–106) concentrates on household design (look out for Salvador Dali's sofa in the shape of Mae West's lips) but also includes toys, textiles and modern graphics. Also don't miss the *Glass Gallery* (Level 4, Room 131), where 4,000 years of glassware is reflected into infinity in a room lined with huge mirrors; the *Fashion Collection* (Level 1, Room 40), with clothes from the 17th and 18th centuries (including wigs, hats, shoes and gloves); or Dior's 'New

The Café

V&A Museum

Open: 10am–5pm

Inexpensive–moderate

Offers a wide range of hot and cold food and delicious cakes (though a bit pricey). Main meals are half-price for children under 10.

The Garden Café

V&A Museum

Open: summer 11.30am–4.30pm

Nice for drinks and snacks on a sunny day.

La Brasserie

272 Brompton Road, SW3

Tel: (020) 7584 1668

Open: Mon–Sat 8am–midnight, Sun 9am–midnight

Expensive

Moderately priced French food. When it's quiet you can just have tea and coffee. Pleasant surroundings.

Chandelier, entrance hall, V&A Museum

Look' – including the latest items to hit the catwalks, including outfits by Vivienne Westwood and Jean Muir.

Some of the rooms, such as the *Morris, Gamble* and *Poynter* rooms on Level 1 (which house a popular café), are worth visiting for their own sakes. *The Morris Room* is especially stunning, decked out with ornate tilework designed by William Morris.

Brompton Oratory (10 mins)

Thurloe Place, Brompton Road, SW7
Tel: *(020) 7808 0900;*
www.bromptonoratory.com
Open: *Mon–Sat 6.30am–8pm*
Sun mass (sung Latin) 11am
Adm: *by donation*

This lavish neo-Baroque church (almost next door to the V&A) was built In 1880–84, for the London Oratory, part of an institute founded by St Philip Neri in Rome in the 16th century. Herbert Gribble designed the building after the Oratorian Chiesa Nuova in Rome. Inside there is an impressive high altar showing scenes from the life of St Philip Neri, massive marble statues of the apostles by Giuseppe Mazzuoli the elder, and European church art dating from the 16th–18th centuries. In

The Oratory

232 Brompton Road, SW3

Tel: (020) 7584 3493

Open: daily noon–10.30pm

Moderate

Set back from the main road with outside seating in the summer time, offering a range of reasonably priced snacks and meals. Helpful waiters. Child friendly.

the Chapel of St Philip Neri a wax effigy of the saint lies covered beneath the altar; he gets shown off on Tuesdays.

Science Museum (11 mins)

Exhibition Road, SW7
Tel: *0870 870 4868;*
www.sciencemuseum.org.uk
Open: *daily 10am–6pm*
Adm: *free, but charges for IMAX (adults £7.50, concs £6), simulator rides (adults £2.50–3.75, concs £1.50–2.75) and some special exhibitions*
Gift shop, bookshop, 4 cafés (ground floor, basement and 3rd floor)
Wheelchair accessible

With the opening of the £48-million Wellcome Wing, the Science Museum launched itself into the 21st century. Set over four floors and bathed in futuristic blue light, state-of-the-art exhibits and multimedia offer bags of hands-on fun and interactivity. The ground floor has regularly changing exhibits based around what's hot in the world of science, plus an IMAX film theatre with a screen as high as five double-decker buses. Would-be Flash Gordons can take a trip to Mars or join the crew aboard a motion simulator before exploring the other floors, which cover human identity, the impact of digital technology and the ways in which science may shape our future. Though impressive, the new wing feels rather sterile when compared with the older parts of the museum. They now have a handy inter-active screens to help navigate the five floors, and are looking better than ever. All the old favourites are here including the traditional push-me-pull-you buttons and levers, pops, bangs and whizzes, and the impressive hardware.

'Making the Modern World', back on the ground floor, is an presentation of old exhibits covering the period 1750–2000, which includes Stephenson's Rocket, a Model-T Ford, a V2 missile and the Apollo 10 command module. Next you come to *'Space'*, where you can find out about the space race and the future of stellar

There are several cafés, restaurants and picnic areas at the Science Museum:

Revolution café

Ground floor, Energy Hall

Open: daily 10am–5.30pm

Inexpensive

A self-service restaurant offering sandwiches, salads, hot dishes and homemade cake.

Deep Blue Café

Ground floor, Wellcome Wing

Family restaurant, awarded Best Restaurant for Kids by the *Observer Food Monthly Awards 2005*. Includes activity boxes. A healthy children menu is on offer; other dishes include pizza and pasta.

Eat Drink Shop

Basement, next to the Terrace

Family snacks, including hot dogs, sandwiches, ice cream, confectionery and drinks. Also for picnics.

Gallery Café

3rd floor, opposite flight lab

Open: holidays only

Tuck shop offering drinks, sandwiches and sweets.

exploration, and have a go at designing your own rocket using a computer. From here, head down the stairs to the basement where *'The Secret Life of the Home'* takes a humorous look at domestic gadgets and gizmos, from vacuum cleaners and washing machines to loos, fridges and heaters. The rest of the basement is given over to activities for younger children.

There is far too much to see in a single day so plan your visit – check out the map of the museum on the ground floor, which also contains some of its most treasured exhibits. Among attractions that should not be missed are: *'Challenge of Materials'* (1st floor), an interactive-rich exhibit exploring the uses and production of manmade products; *'Flight'* (3rd floor), with all manner of planes, rockets and engines, including a Spitfire, a Messerschmitt and a Doodlebug; and a nausea-inducing Motionride simulator (3rd floor), which emulates a flight in a Harrier Jump Jet.

Before heading for the shop, make time, for the 1903 Harle Syke mill engine on the ground floor. This pillar-box-red monster could power 1,700 looms in its day. Two engineers are now permanently on hand to keep it running and answer questions. It never goes above quarter speed for fear of shaking the building to its foundations.

The Science Museum

Royal Albert Hall (15 mins)

Kensington Gore, SW7
Tel: *(020) 7838 3105: www.royalalberthall.com,
www.bbc.co.uk/proms*
Open: *tours Fri–Tue, first at 10am, last at
3.30pm; duration 45 mins (begin at door 12 on
Prince Consort Rd)*
Adm: *adults £6, children 5–16 £3.50,
concessions £3–5, family £16*
Wheelchair accessible

The Royal Albert Hall was built as a memorial to Prince Albert, the beloved husband of Queen Victoria from 1840 until his death from typhoid fever in 1861 (as was the *Albert Memorial*, across the road in Hyde Park, *see* p.84). The domed, circular hall, one of the grandest Victorian buildings in London, can seat 8,000 in the auditorium and was paid for by public donation. Additional capital was raised by selling 1,300 of the seats at £100 each for every first night performance for 999 years.

These days the hall is in constant use for concerts from pop to classical, the odd tennis match and, most famously, for the Proms, a series of classical music concerts held each summer, founded by conductor Henry Wood in 1895. The concerts reflect a wide range of international musical tastes and trends, as well as complete opera

Café Consort

*Royal Albert Hall
(door 12 to south
porch)*

Tel: (020) 7589 8212

*Open: Mon–Fri
8.30 am–4pm,
Sat-Sun 10am-4pm*

Moderate

Light lunches and a selection of hot dishes. The café is also licensed

The RAH has two other restaurants, the **Elgar Room** (door 8 to circle level) and the **Victoria Restaurant** (door 1 to Circle level) which is open two hours before performances begin. Reservations recommended:

Tel: (020) 7589 8212

The Royal Albert Hall

Bibendum

Michelin House, 81 Fulham Road, SW3

Tel: (020) 7581 5817; www.bibendum.co.uk

Open: Mon–Fri noon–2.30pm and 7–11.30pm, Sat 12.30–3pm and 7–11.30pm, Sun 7–10.30pm only

Expensive

One of London's trendy dining places. A little on the pricy side – but you are paying for top chefs and a classic Art Noveau venue in which to dine.

Cactus Blue

86 Fulham Road, SW3

Tel: (020) 7395 5801

Open: Mon–Fri 5.30–11.45pm, Sat–Sun noon–11.45pm

Expensive

American southwestern nosh. Hot and spicy dishes served in this hip Tex-Mex eatery.

Harvey Nichols Fifth Floor Restaurant

Tel: (020) 7235 5250

Open: Lunch Mon-Thu noon–3pm, Fri noon–3.30pm; Sat noon-6pm; and Sun Dinner: Mon–Sat 6pm-11pm

Expensive

Seriously stylish eatery–the place to see and be seen.

performances and specially commissioned contemporary works. On the Last Night of the Proms (in early September) the orchestra belts out patriotic melodies such as Elgar's 'Pomp and Circumstance' (*Land of Hope and Glory*) and Henry Wood's arrangement 'Fantasia on British Sea Songs', and the excited audience bobs, conducts and sings along with great gusto.

The Fulham Road (6 mins)

South of the station you will find the lower end of the Fulham Road. Notable amid the upmarket clothes and antique shops in the area is the Conran Shop (no.81), an upmarket version of Sir Terence Conran's Habitat (*see* p.126). He opened it in the 1960s, almost single-handedly transforming the British interior overnight with his range of simple, affordable and well-designed household goods. Even if you don't buy anything, it is worth going just to see **Michelin House**, a witty Art Noveau palace designed by the French architect F. Espinasse as an advert for the Michelin tyre company. Note the corners of the building, capped with the bulbous stacks of 'tyres' which light up to form the torso of the Michelin Man.

KNIGHTSBRIDGE

Harvey Nichols (1 min)

109–125 Knightsbridge, SW1
Tel: *(020) 7235 5000; www.harveynichols.com*
Open: *Mon–Fri 10am–8pm, Sat 10am–7pm, Sun noon–6pm*
Restaurant, bar and café; Wheelchair accessible

Harvey Nichols was founded by Benjamin Harvey in 1813 as a linen shop. Preposterously fashionable and known by its clientèle as 'Harvey Nicks', amid the picture-perfect displays you'll find the latest catwalk mens- and ladieswear, desperately funky accessories, 'must-have' beauty products and homewares – including porcelain hand-decorated bowls and lambswool blankets for your pets.

Harrods (4 mins)

87–135 Brompton Road, SW1
***Tel**: (020) 7730 1234*
***Open**: Mon– Sat 10am–8pm, Sun noon–6pm*
16 restaurants, bars and cafés
Wheelchair accessible

Henry Charles Harrod, a tea merchant from Eastcheap, founded his small grocer's shop in Knightsbridge in 1849. Today Harrods is a mecca for shoppers and tourists, and is owned by Mohammed Al Fayed, who bought it from House of Fraser for £615 million in 1985.

You could spend the whole day here quite happily. The pet department is especially good and usually proves a hit with children (time was you could order any animal in the world from here – even an elephant). The toy department on the 4th floor will also keep kids amused for hours. If you're feeling peckish, Planet Harrods, with its gloopy shakes and burgers, is a good stop-off point. Don't miss the food halls (all seven of them, including a fabulous hall of chocolate), where the extravagance of the food displays is rivalled only by the lustre of the Edwardian Art Noveau tiling depicting hunting scenes.

At any time of the year, Harrods is one of London's big attractions but in the run-up

Bar Fifth Floor

Tel: (020) 7235 5250

Open: Mon–Sat 11am–11pm; Sun noon–6pm

Moderate

Sophisticated with very good cocktails

Café

Tel: (020) 7823 1839

Open: Mon–Sat 10am–10.30pm; Sun 11am–6pm

Moderate

More informal option than the restaurant.

Shopping at Harrods, Brompton Road

Gloriette Patisserie

128 Brompton Road, SW3

Tel: (020) 7589 4750

Open: Mon–Sat 7am–7pm, Sun 9am–6pm

Inexpensive

Sticky Austrian cakes and sweets, salads and sandwiches. Good coffee, and it's child-friendly.

Monza

6 Yeoman's Row, SW3

Tel: (020) 7591 0210

Open: 7pm–11.30pm daily, Tue–Sun noon–2.30pm

Moderate

Family-orientated, friendly little Italian restaurant serving mouthwatering pizza, pasta and seafood dishes. Reasonably priced.

Hard Rock Café

150 Old Park Lane, W1

Tel: (020) 7629 0382; www.hardrock.com

Open: Mon–Thurs 11.30am–12am, Fri–Sat 11.30am–1am, Sun 11.30am–11.30pm; also daily for breakfast 8–11am

Moderate

Buzzing restaurant for all ages, decorated with rock memorabilia such as a jacket once owned by John Lennon and Jimi Hendrix's and Eric Clapton's guitars. The menu is fresh tex-mex, steaks and burgers and there are often queues to get in, but it's worth the wait.

to Christmas every shop window becomes a pantomime in miniature and the food halls are piled high. The famous sale in January is something of a tradition, with people queuing all night to join the ritual stampede for top-quality bargains. While not as exclusive as it once was, Harrods may still refuse entry to those sporting large backpacks or what might otherwise be considered inappropriate dress

HYDE PARK CORNER

Apsley House, The Wellington Museum (2 mins)

149 Piccadilly, W1
Tel: *(020) 7499 5676*
Open: *Tue–Sun 11am–5pm*
Adm: *adult £4.50, concessions £3, under-18s free; Wheelchair access to some public areas*

As a reward for finishing off Napoleon at the Battle of Waterloo in 1815, the Duke of Wellington was given this house at no.149 Piccadilly. Although he was delighted with his gift, he was less impressed with the address and promptly dubbed it Number One, London. A lover of art, Wellington amassed a sizeable collection during his stay here, from 1817 until his death in 1852, which included many paintings and precious objects given to him by influential figures, as well as the spoils of war. His descendants still live here but 10 rooms have been restored and are open to the public. Paintings by great masters, such as Goya, Rubens and Velázquez, silver and gold plate and priceless porcelain are on show, as is the unmissable Canova – a 3.35-m (11-ft) statue of a nude Napoleon, which towers over the grand staircase.

Constitution Arch (4 mins)

Hyde Park Corner, SW1
Tel: *(020) 7930 2726; www.english-heritage.org.uk*
Open: *Apr–Oct Wed–Sun 10am–5pm, Nov–Mar Wed–Sun 10am–4pm*
Adm: *adults £3, children £1.50, concessions*

*£2.30 (joint ticket with Apsley House
£6/4.20/3, family £15)*
Gift shop; Wheelchair accessible

This stone arch was designed by Decimus
Burton and stood from 1846–82 opposite
the main entrance to Hyde Park. It was
originally crowned by a gigantic 40-ton
bronze equestrian statue of the Duke of
Wellington, hero and statesman. In 1882,
the statue and the arch were both moved –
the statue (ridiculed for its bulk) to
Aldershot and the arch to here. The statue
was replaced by the present 'Quadriga' by
Adrian Jones (a former cavalry officer), in
1912. The sculpture sees a boy driving the
horses of the quadriga (four-horse war
chariot) as Peace descends on them. Inside
the arch are three floors of exhibits on past
functions of the arch (including its use as a
tiny police station), London's statues and
memorials, and a history of blue plaques.
There are marvellous views of Hyde Park
from the viewing platforms under the
sculpture. A unit from either the Blues and
Royals or the Household Cavalry pass
thiough the arch at 10.45am on their route
to the Changing of the Guard at
Horseguards Parade (*see* p.75).

Hard Rock Café

150 Old Park Lane, W1

*Tel: (020) 7629 0382;
www.hardrock.com*

*Open: Mon–Thurs
11.30am–12am,
Fri–Sat
11.30am–1am, Sun
11.30am–11.30pm;
also daily for
breakfast 8–11am*

Moderate

Buzzing restaurant
for all ages,
decorated with rock
memorabilia such
as a jacket once
owned by John
Lennon and Jimi
Hendrix's and Eric
Clapton's guitars.
The menu is fresh
tex-mex, steaks and
burgers and there
are often queues to
get in, but it's worth
the wait.

GREEN PARK

see **Victoria line, p.167**

Green Park p.167, The Ritz p.168, Royal Academy of Arts p.169, Fortnum and Mason's p.170, Faraday Museum p.170, Spencer House p.171

Rainforest Café

20–24 Shaftesbury Avenue, W1

Tel: (020) 7434 3111; www.therainforest cafe.co.uk

Open: Mon–Fri noon–10pm, Sat 11.30am–7.45pm, Sun and school hols 11.30am–10pm

Expensive

The food, burgers, fries, gloopy milkshakes and ice-cream sundaes, are alright but it is the décor that you come for – cascading waterfalls, dense Amazonian foliage and robotic forest animals. Kids love it. You may have to queue.

The bottom of Regent's Street, running into Piccadilly Circus

PICCADILLY CIRCUS

Piccadilly Circus was created in 1819 but took its name from Pikadilly Hall, the home of Robert Baker, who was famous in the 17th century for selling a type of collar known as a 'piccadill'. It lost its circular form in 1886 when Shaftesbury Avenue was built.

The centrepiece is a fountain dating from 1893, whose winged figure ready to shoot an absent arrow from his bow, is known as **Eros**, after the God of Love. It actually represents the Angel of Christian Charity , since the fountain was erected in memory of the Victorian philanthropist, Lord Shaftesbury.

Piccadilly Circus is the junction for five major streets, Shaftsbury Avenue and Haymarket, home to several London theatres, Regent's Street and Oxford Street, and Piccadilly, which heads down to Green Park (*see* p.167). Head down the Haymarket and you will reach Pall Mall, which is full of private clubs such as the Athenaeum and the Reform, and if you go down the steps at the end, you get to the Mall (*see* p.74).

London Trocadero (2 mins)

1 Piccadilly Circus, W1
(main entrance on Coventry St)
Tel: *(020) 7734 2777*
www.londontrocadero.com
Open: *daily 10–12am, Fri–Sat until 1am*
Adm: *free to building, charges for rides and activities; Restricted wheelchair access*
Here you will find six floors of video games, virtual-reality rides, pool tables, ten-pin bowling and bumper cars, as well as numerous burger bars and a cyber café. All this is set in a futuristic, if somewhat dowdy, environment known as Funland, which children will, no doubt, enjoy and adults will tolerate.

St James's Church, Piccadilly (3mins)

197 Piccadilly, W1
Tel: *(020) 7734 4511*
Open: *8–7 daily*
Adm: *free*

Although Christopher Wren worked on many of London's churches, patching them up after the Great Fire of London in 1666, this is the only one that he built from scratch. It proved one of his favourites, 'I think it may be found beautiful and convenient' he later wrote. After the bustle and noise of Piccadilly, the church is a restful place. The free lunchtime recitals are also a good reason to visit, as is the flea market (Wed–Sun), antiques market (Tue) and the café in the annexe.

Planet Hollywood

13 Coventry Street, W1

Tel: (020) 7437 7639; www.planethollywoodlondon.com

Open: Mon–Thu 11.30am–2am, Fri–Sat 11.30am–3am, Sun 11.30am–12.30am

Expensive

Burgers and fries, milkshakes, the lot! Plus Hollywood memorabilia and a gift shop.

⬤ LEICESTER SQUARE

see **Northern line, p.26**

⬤ COVENT GARDEN

Modern-day Covent Garden was part of a Saxon trading port until the 9th century and was agricultural land until the 17th. the name comes from 'Convent' Garden as it once belonged to Westminster Abbey (*see* p.92). In the 18th century, you came to Covent Garden for a good time. The happy mix of market stalls, gambling dens, coffee houses and Turkish baths (many of which were brothels) and rowdy pubs, attracted literary types, such as Henry Fielding, James Boswell, Richard Sheridan and Alexander Pope, who came looking for inspiration.

In the 19th century, Covent Garden became London's wholesale vegetable, fruit and flower market, famous as the setting for Bernard Shaw's play, *Pygmalion* (and the film version, *My Fair Lady*). The italianate portico of **St Paul's Church**, built by Inigo Jones in 1633 just south of the market, is where Eliza first meets Henry Higgins. It is now known as the actors' church and has memorials to many screen legends, including Noel Coward, Charlie Chaplin and Vivien Leigh.

In 1974 the market moved out to Vauxhall and the central market was deserted until 1980, when it reopened as a respectable, pedestrianized piazza with shops, stalls, some decent museums and plenty of places to eat *al fresco*. Now the streets around are also filled with trendy shops and eateries (*see* below).

St Paul's Church,
Covent Garden Piazza

Covent Garden is also the best place to see London's street entertainers, where they perform near the Tube, in the market and in front of St Paul's Church. At weekends crowds gather to watch jugglers, fire-eaters, mime artists and other entertainers.

Covent Garden Shopping

Some of the more unusual or specialist shops in Covent Garden are described below. Most shops are open daily, often until 7pm or later from Monday to Saturday, and on Sunday from around 11am to 6pm.

In the Market and Piazza are the **Apple Market** (North Hall), with handmade British arts, crafts, clothes and on Mondays, specifically, antiques; Benjamin Pollock's Toy Shop (44 The Market), with old-fashioned toys and teddies; Culpeper the Herbalist (8 The Market), selling medicial herbs, spices, oils and fine foods, mostly from organic sources; Godiva (17 The Piazza), a luxury Belgian chocolatier; Lyle & Scott (40 King Street), with authentic Scottish knitwear, in lambswool and cashmere, including vintage and golfing ranges; and Segar & Snuff Parlour (27a The Market), with all the discerning smoker could wish for, including hand-rolled Cuban cigars.

Floral Street has Paul Smith (nos. 40–44), a high-quality, typically English designer for

Belgo Centraal

50 Earlham Street, WC2

Tel: 0871 223 8059; www.belgo-restaurants.com

Open: Mon–Sat noon–11.30, Sun 10am–10.30

Moderate

A short walk from the tube, this Belgian themed restaurant has a good range of beers and wonderful portions, especially of *moules et frites*, lobster and salads. Reasonably priced, but its underground location and accoustics can make it noisy in the evenings.

The Apple Market, Covent Garden Market

Carluccio's

29a Neal Street, WC2

Tel: (020) 7240 1487 (shop), 7836 8368 (restaurant); www.carluccios.com

Open: Mon–Fri 8am–7pm, Sat 11am–7pm, Sun noon–6pm

Expensive

Italian café and next-door food store run by the famous chef Antonio Carluccio, offering high-quality regional Italian food.

Food for Thought

31 Neal Street, WC2

Tel: (020) 7836 9072

Open: Mon–Sat noon–8.15pm, Sun noon–4pm

Inexpensive

This tiny Covent Garden institution has possibly the best vegetarian food in London.

Neal's Yard Bakery

6 Neal's Yard, WC2

Tel: (020) 7836 5199

Open: Mon–Sat 10.30am–5pm

Inexpensive

Organic cakes, vegetarian and vegan savouries and wholefoods.

adults and children clothes and homeware, perfumes and accessories; and the Tintin Shop (no. 34) is solely devoted to the Belgian boy-detective and his pals.

In **Long Acre** and the roads leading off it are Muji (35 Long Acre), the Japanese Woolworth's, selling inexpensive and well-designed homeware, clothes, stationery and storage; Stanfords (12–14 Long Acre), the specialist map and travel bookshop, founded in 1853; Snow & Rock (4 Mercer Street), with outdoor clothing and sports equipment and a café and an in-store sports rehab clinic.

In **Neal Street** and the roads leading off it are American Classics (20 Endell Street), with classic and authentic American clothing; the Astrology Shop (78 Neal Street), where you can buy a personal horoscope, birth charts, astrology books and other related items; Birkenstock (70 Neal Street), selling those ugly-cute bowl-soles in a multitude of styles; the Kite Store (48 Neal Street), selling traditional kites to the latest hi-tech stunt models; the Natural Shoe Store (21 Neal Street), with comfortable shoes that have a pleasing albeit hippyish touch; Neal's Yard Dairy (17 Shorts Gardens), a mecca for traditional British produce and cheeses, many of which are matured on site; Neal's Yard Remedies (15 Neal's Yard), with herbal, homeopathic and aromatherapeutic remedies, and therapy rooms (2 Neal's Yard, tel: (020) 7379 7662) offering alternative treatments for various health problems; Skate of Mind (Thomas Neal Centre, Earlham Street), for everything a skateboarder could ever want; and the Tea House (15 Neal Street), a temple to fine teas and infusions, with a huge range of blends and teapots.

Seven Dials has the Dover Bookshop (18 Earlham Street), a wonderful shop that sells copyright-free images and references in book form; Dress Circle (57–59 Monmouth Street), selling a wide selection of musical theatre and showbiz products, and collectables; and Grosvenor Prints, which has a huge stock of antique prints, dating from the 17th to early 20th century.

Other quirky shops include the Australia Shop (27 Maiden Lane), with everything homesick Australians might miss, from Vegemite to Driza-Bone clothing; The Cinema Store (4b Orion House, Upper St Martin's Lane), with cinema collectables, from vintage and contemporary posters to soundtracks – they can get their hands on most movie-related items; and Stanley Gibbons (399 The Strand), founded in 1856, a magnet for international philatelists and has literally millions of stamps, and loads of reference books and associated stamp-collecting paraphernalia on sale.

Royal Opera House (1 min)

Bow Street (main entrance), WC2
Tel: *(020) 7304 4000; www.roh.org.uk*
Open: *Front of house areas daily 10am–3pm; box office open Mon–Sat 10am–8pm*
Backstage guided tours: *Mon–Sat 10.30am, 12.30pm and 2.30pm (lasts 75–90 mins); adults £8, concessions £7*
10 bars and restaurants; Wheelchair accessible (although not for all of the tour)

The first two theatres on this site burnt down in 1808 and 1856. The third, designed by Edward Barry (whose father built the Houses of Parliament), reopened in 2000 after an extensive and expensive (£214 million) refurbishment. The Royal Opera House, also home to the Royal Ballet, is doing its best to justify the huge cost of rebuilding with a new policy of easy access, which includes tours, exhibitions, cheaper tickets and free lunchtime concerts. Also, you do not now need to buy an opera ticket to visit the ROH's new bar and restaurant or to sit out on the sunny terrace, which overlooks Covent Garden's Piazza.

London's Transport Museum (3 mins)

Covent Garden Piazza, WC2
Tel: *(020) 7565 7299 or 7379 6344*
www.ltmuseum.co.uk
Open: *Sat–Thu 10am–6pm, Fri 11am–6pm (last adm 5.15pm)*
Adm: *adults £5.95, concessions £4.50, under-16s free; Gift shop; Wheelchair accessible*

Paul Boulangerie & Patisserie

29–30 Bedford Street, WC2

Tel: (020) 7836 3304; www.paul.fr

Open: Mon–Fri 7.30am–9pm, Sat–Sun 9am–9pm

Moderate

Fantastic bakers from the French chain, selling scrumptious breads and pastries. The desserts are mouthwatering, with crunch pastry bases that you only get from France. The café at the rear often has queues, but it's worth waiting for a seat.

Amphitheatre Restaurant

Royal Opera House, Top Floor

Tel: (020) 7212 9254

Open: 11.30am–2.30pm

Expensive

Evening entry only available to opera-goers. Open from 1 hour before the performance.

Housed in Covent Garden's former Flower Market, the London Transport Museum is every transport buff's dream, with an unrivalled collection of horse-drawn trams, buses, trolley cars and Tube carriages dating from the 1830s onwards. The coaches and buses, including London's first double-decker, are beautifully restored and you can step inside later examples. Early film, sound-effects of clip-clopping horses and models of passengers in period costume al lsummon up a sense of the times.

The making of the Underground is well documented. There are early carriages in which you can sit, special exhibits on tunnelling, tickets and station design, and biographies of the movers and shakers in London Underground's history, including Harry Beck, who designed the Tube map.

The museum is extremely child-friendly with lots of screens to touch and 15 hands-on zones that kids can work their way round, punching a special ticket at each point, learning about London Transport as they go. In addition they can drive a Tube train (this is fun for adults too) or take a ride in the Fun Bus (under-5s only). In the Fast Forward section they can play with computers that look at the future of transport in London. Costumed actors, including a horse-dung collector (1,000 tons of dung were deposited each day when horses worked for London Transport),

London's Transport Museum

a World War I bus cleaner and a 1930s tram driver, are on hand to give visitors the benefit of their years of experience.

Theatre Museum (3 mins)

Tavistock Street (entrance off Russell Street), WC2
Tel: *(020) 7943 4700; www.theatremuseum.org*
Open: *Tue–Sun 10am–6pm;* **Adm**: *free*
Guided tours: *Tue–Sun at 11am, 2pm and 4pm*
Wheelchair accessible; ring for special exhibitions
Workshops for aspirant actors and free
makeup displays (call or see website for info)

A must for anyone interested in the stage, this little museum, housed in art of the original flower market, reviews the history of the English theatre from the opening of Britain's first playhouse (in 1576) to the rise of the National Theatre and beyond. Special exhibitions are devoted to topics such as English pantomime or Hamlet through the ages, and there is also a collection of memorabilia, including costumes, props used by famous actors, countless playbills and posters and early drafts of well-known plays. The museum is engagingly hands-on with makeup and costume workshops, giving kids and adults alike the chance to dress up. Fancy yourself as a werewolf? Or Snow White? The museum is a bit

Theatre Museum,

disorganized so the lively guided tour by a professional actor – free of any additional charge – is highly recommended.

HOLBORN

see **Central line, p.39**
Sir John Soane's Museum p.39

Dickens House Museum

RUSSELL SQUARE

Dickens House Museum (9 mins)
48 Doughty Street, WC1
***Tel**: (020) 7405 2127; www.dickensmuseum.com*
***Open**: Mon–Sat 10am–5pm, Sun 11am–5pm*
***Adm**: adults £5, children £3, concessions £4, family £14. Some wheelchair access*

The novelist Charles Dickens lived here from 1837 to 1839, during which time he polished off the last six, monthly instalments of *The Pickwick Papers* and wrote and published *Oliver Twist* and *Nicholas Nickleby*. There is an abundance of memorabilia, including portraits, letters, the quill pen Dickens used when composing his last unfinished novel, a turquoise engagement ring he gave to his wife in 1836, the tall desk at which he wrote his novels (standing up), a monogrammed silver nail clipper, and the bars from the Marshalsea Prison where his father was once jailed for non-payment of debt.

KING'S CROSS ST PANCRAS

see **Northern Line, p.110**
London Canal Museum p.110

The British Library

VICTORIA LINE

The Victoria Line is the baby of the London Underground and was opened in stages between 1968 and 1971. Originally proposed as 'Route C' in 1948, this line would never have been built had not the government been looking for a job creation scheme to ease unemployment in the north of England. The 14-mile route has 16 stations and cost £91 million (an astronomical figure for the time). Serving four main railway stations (Victoria, Euston, St Pancras and King's Cross), and passing through London's three busiest Underground stations (Victoria, Oxford Circus and King's Cross/St Pancras), the Victoria Line was very soon carrying passengers at the rate of 58 million a year. Today this figure has risen to 165.5 million passengers annually.

KINGS CROSS ST PANCRAS

See Northern Line (Bank branch), p.110

London Canal Museum p.110

EUSTON

St Pancras New Church (6 mins)

Euston Road (corner of Upper Woburn Place), NW1
Tel: *(020) 7388 1461; www.stpancraschurch.org*
Open: *Mon 9am–12pm, Wed–Sat 9.30am–6pm,*
Sun 9.30am–12pm and 4pm–6.30pm
(service 10am)

It is said that there has been a church to St
Pancras near here since AD405, 10 years after
14-year-old Pancras was killed in Rome for
refusing to worship Dionysus. Old St Pancras
Church stands on the spot just behind the
station (Pancras Road) and is thought to be
one of the oldest Christian sites in Britain.
However, by the beginning of the 19th century,
it had fallen into decay and a new church was
consecrated in 1822 on the corner of Upper
Woburn Place. Built by Henry William and
William Inwood and costing £89,296, it was
the most expensive London church to be built
since Wren's St Paul's Cathedral (*see* p.44). They
modelled it on the ancient Athenian Temple of
the Erechtheion, on the Acropolis; at its east
end there are two caryatid porches guarding
the entrance to the crypt (you can see one of
the original caryatids in the British Museum,
see p.37). Unfortunately a mistake was made

Caryatid portico,
St Pancras Church

162

Entrance to the British Library

and the figures were too tall to fit the space – a problem solved by cutting out 12ins from their midriffs, which is why they now look a little odd! The tower, above the enormous Ionic portico, was inspired by the Athenian 'Tower of the Winds'. Inside, the pulpit was made from a famous old tree, the Fairlop Oak, which grew in Hainault Forest, Essex, and was blown down in 1820. It was said to 'have existed from halfway up the Christian era', and the width of its trunk was 9m (30ft).

British Library (11 mins)

St Pancras, 96 Euston Road, NW1
Tel: *(020) 7412 7332; www.bl.uk*
Open: *Mon and Wed–Fri 9.30am–6pm, Tue 9.30am–8pm, Sat 9.30am–5pm, Sun 11am–5pm*
Adm: *free, though donations are welcome*
Tours, exhibitions, restaurant, cafés
Wheelchair accessible

Until 1998 the British Library was part of the British Museum (**see** p.37) and most of it wasn't open to the public. Now in a new building, there is greater access, although access to the reading rooms remains by permit only. Containing some 18 million volumes, this is one of the biggest libraries in the world. You can admire its vast stamp collection or listen to part of its sound archive via a 1950s Wurlitzer-style jukebox on the upper ground floor, but the best place to head for is the *Treasures of the British Library*. Here you can see such historic items as the beautifully illuminated *Lindisfarne Gospels* (c. AD 700), one of the four surviving copies of the *Magna Carta* (1215) and the first ever printed bible, known as the *Gutenberg Bible* (1455). In addition there is an illuminated version of Chaucer's *Canterbury Tales*; Shakespeare's *First Folio* (the first collected edition of his plays); the '*Codex Arundel*', a collection of notes by Leonardo da Vinci (1452–1519); and literary works, in their own handwriting, by the likes of Ben Jonson, Andrew Marvell, Jane Austen, Charles Dickens, George Eliot and Virgina Woolf.

More up-to-date exhibits include some of the original Beatles' lyrics to songs such as 'Ticket to Ride' and 'Michelle', written on bits of scrap paper and envelopes. Also, don't miss the interactive *Workshop of Words, Sound and Images*, which traces the story of print and book production from the earliest written documents through to modern digital printing (on Saturdays from 11am onwards there are free demonstrations of bookbinding, calligraphy and printing). The imposing six-storey tower, next to the café/restaurant, houses a 65,000-volume collection, that once belonged to George III.

⬤ OXFORD CIRCUS

Oxford Street (1 min)

Oxford Street was once the road to Oxford, and was built over the site of a Roman road that ran from Hampshire to the Suffolk coast. It became the shopping street it is now in the late 19th century, when the first department stores, such as Selfridges, (*see* p.35), were established.

Dover Castle

43 Weymouth Mews, W1

Tel: (020) 7580 4412

Open: Mon–Fri 11.30am–11pm, Sat noon–11

Inexpensive

Inviting little pub, tucked away in a mews.

Shopping along Oxford Street

Ozer

4–5 Langham Place, W1

Tel: (020) 7323 0505

Open: daily noon–2.30pm and 6–11pm

Moderate

A Turkish and North African menu offered amidst candlelight and red velvet; the red lentil soup and lamb in kumquat and limequat marmalade are delicious.

Strada

15–16 New Burlington Street, W1

Tel: (020) 7287 5967; www.strada.co.uk

Open: Mon–Sat noon–midnight, Sun noon–10.30pm

Moderate

Branch of the marvellous London chain, serving simple but mouthwatering Italian food. Crispy pizza is cooked in the wood-fired oven, and all dishes are cooked with fresh ingredients (try the *linguine alla pescatora*). Still water is complementary, service is always excellent and children are welcome.

Oxford Street is 1.5 miles long, so don't expect to get round every shop in one day or you will expire in the attempt. Much of it consists of chains that you'll find elsewhere in the UK; you'll find it more worthwhile to visit the large flagship-type shops for their vast ranges. John Lewis, the River Island flagship store, Debenhams and House of Fraser are all a short walk west from the station. On the circus itself are the NikeTown store, Benetton and H&M. Eastwards lies Topshop's flagship store, Borders, Marks & Spencer, Urban Outfitters, the massive flagships of music and home entertainment, HMV and Virgin. The quality of shops decreases as you get nearer Tottenham Court Road.

Regent Street (1 min)

Beautiful Regent Street was built by John Nash in the early 19th century to connect Regent's Park to Carlton House and thereby improve the profitability of the surrounding land, which was owned by the Crown. Today it's Oxford Street's upmarket sister, with shops such as Dickens & Jones, **Liberty** (*see* below), Burberry, Jaeger, Viyella, Swarovski, Hackett, Mappin & Webb, **Hamley's** (*see* below), Wedgwood, Boodle & Dunthorne, Aquascutum and Austin Reed. However, several shop leases on Regent Street will run out within the next few years. The Crown Estates, which still owns the buildings, has embarked on a £500 million development and many of the shops are likely to change; newcomers such as the Apple Store, which opened in 2004, will have more space to play with so it's likely the smaller, more exclusive names may head elsewhere.

Liberty (4 mins)

214–220 Regent Street, W1
***Tel**: (020) 7734 1234; www.liberty.co.uk*
***Open**: Mon–Wed and Fri–Sat 10am–7pm, Thu 10am–8pm, Sun noon–6pm*
Wheelchair from Regent Street entrance

One of London's most famous department stores, Liberty began in the 19th century as

Liberty

an outlet for the Arts and Crafts movement selling, among other things, silks, fabrics and wallpaper designed by the poet and craftsman William Morris (**see** p.185). The Tudor-style exterior and rich wooden panelling inside, together with the warren-like layout full of inviting nooks and crannies, make it an intriguing place to shop. Kitchenware, women's fashion, jewellery and accessories are especially good (though expensive). On the top floor you can still buy antique Arts and Crafts furniture.

Hamley's (5 mins)

188–196 Regent Street, W1
Tel: (020) 7734 3161; www.hamleys.com
Open: Mon–Fri 10am–8pm, Sat 9.30am–8pm, Sun noon–6pm; Wheelchair accessible

Hamleys is a tourist attraction in its own right and the most famous children's toyshop in London. As soon as you walk through the doors you realize you're in for something special as demonstrators buzz you with low-flying planes, blow bubbles or construct miniature masterpieces from balloons. Set over six floors, you can easily spend half a day here trying out the latest toys and games, fiddling with the Lego® and racing the Scalextrix® cars at top speed round a mini Brands Hatch. The kids may like it too.

Carnaby Street (6 mins)
www.carnaby.co.uk
Walking time: 6 mins

Gone are the days when you might have seen anyone on Carnaby Street wearing a kaftan or Mary Quant clothes. After several years spent in the doldrums of tourist-shop hell, Carnaby Street has had a new burst of life injected into it, with shiny, trendy shops for smart 20-somethings and teenagers. The marketing mob have rebranded 'Carnaby', which today covers several streets as well as the original Swingster – Foubert Street, Ganton Street, Kingly Street, Kingly Court, Broadwick Street and Newburgh Street all have shops worth peering into, such as The Dispensary, All Saints, Miss Sixty, Diesel, Michiko Koshino, Jess James, MAC and Pixi.

GREEN PARK

Green Park (1 min)
www.royalparks.gov.uk
Open: *daily*

This area was enclosed by Henry VIII and turned into a Royal Park by Charles II. It is not one of the capital's most interesting

Green Park

open spaces but, with acres of well-tended lawns, shady plane and lime trees, cast-iron benches, deckchairs for hire and quaint old gas lamps, it is a lovely place to relax. Green Park was originally a leper's burial ground and, as a mark of respect for the dead below, no flowers are planted here. Nevertheless, come Spring, a profusion of daffodils pop up and turn it into a green park with yellow spots. If you walk across it you will come to the Mall and Buckingham Palace (*see* p.74).

The Ritz (2 mins)

150 Piccadilly, W1
Tel: *(020) 7493 8181; www.theritzlondon.com*
Open: *for tea in the Palm Court at 12, 1.30, 3.30 or 5pm*
Wheelchair accessible through Piccadilly entrance

Although you have to be fairly wealthy to stay at this historic hotel, which opened in 1906, afternoon tea, by comparison, seems affordable and is now something of an institution. At £34 per head it is still rather steep but the grandeur of the venue, the politeness of the staff and the sight of the cakes, sandwiches and scones piled high on silver platters make it an experience few are likely to forget. It is a popular treat and you will need to book well in advance (at least three months for a weekend reservation), or you can try your luck at 1.30pm. Also, remember to dress smartly – jacket and tie are compulsory for men, with strictly no jeans or trainers.

Tamarind

20 Queen Street, W1

Tel: (020) 7629 3561

Open: Mon–Sat noon–3pm and 6–11.30pm, Sun noon–3pm and 6–10.30pm

Expensive

Chic and therefore on the pricy side, but this is one of the best Indian restaurants to be found in London. A treat.

Sofra

18 Shepherd Street, W1

Tel: (020) 7493 3320

Open: Daily noon–midnight

Moderate

Delicious Turkish food: fresh mezze dishes, grills and casseroles, with prompt service.

Al Hamra

31–33 Shepherd Market, W1 (Green Park)

Tel: (020) 7493 1954

Open: daily noon–midnight

Expensive

Swanky Lebanese restaurant. It's not cheap, but the food is delicious and spicy.

Academy Restaurant

Open: 10am–5.30pm, 8.30pm on Fri

Inexpensive

Cool new restaurant, offering hot and cold food, in airy mural-painted surroundings.

Royal Academy of Arts (6 mins)

Burlington House, Piccadilly, W1
Tel: *(020) 7300 8000;*
www.royalacademy.org.uk
Open: *daily 10am–6pm, Fri until 10pm (last adm 30 mins before close)*
Adm: *varies according to each exhibition*
Restaurant, café, gift shop
Wheelchair accessible

The Royal Academy's Palladian building was completed in 1720 as the private home for the third Earl of Burlington. It remained a private residence until 1854 when it was bought by the government to house the Royal Academy of Arts. The brainchild of Sir Joshua Reynolds (whose statue, brush and palette in hand, stands in the courtyard), it was the country's first-ever school of art. These days the RA is better known for its temporary exhibitions (past shows have included 'Botticelli's Drawing', 'Rembrandt's Women' and 'Aztecs'). The other big draw is the Summer Exhibition, which attracts huge numbers between May and August. The difference with this exhibition is that it is open to everybody, whether they are famous or unknown. Every year 8,000 new submissions – paintings, sculptures and

Sir Joshua Reynolds, Forecourt of the RA, Burlington House

architectural proposals – are considered by the Academy's judges; about 1,500 of them are accepted for the show.

Fortnum & Mason (6 mins)

181 Piccadilly, W1
Tel: *(020) 7734 8040;*
www.fortnumandmason.com
Open: *Mon–Sat 10am–6.30pm, Sun noon–6pm (Food Hall, Patio Restaurant and Lower Ground Floor only)*

William Fortnum was employed as a footman in the household of George III, and began selling used candles from the royal candelabras to the queen's ladies. He was so successful that he set up a grocery shop with his partner, Hugh Mason, in 1707. Today Fortnum's is still 'Grocers and Provision Merchants' to the Queen and Prince Charles, and runs to six floors selling 'almost every method of pleasing the mind and body', from game pies and rare teas to toys and crystal wares. It's all terribly English and a little unreal, with pristine packaging and equally immaculate staff. Most people come for the food halls on the ground floor, which rival Harrods' in Knightsbridge (*see* p.148).

The delightful handcrafted clock over the main entrance (1964) has mechanical figures of Mr Fortnum holding a candelabra and Mr Mason, who turn and bow to each other on the hour.

Faraday Museum (7 mins)

Royal Institution, 21 Albemarle Street, W1
Tel: *(020) 7409 2992; www.rigb.org*
Open: *Mon–Fri 10am–5pm*
Adm: *adults £1, concessions 50p*
Wheelchair accessible

Michael Faraday, the impoverished son of a country blacksmith, received little formal education and was apprenticed to a bookbinder at the age of 14. During this time he took the opportunity to read some of the books brought in for rebinding. One article on electricity in an edition of the *Encyclopaedia Britannica* particularly fascinated him. Using old bottles and bits

Fortnum & Mason's
Fountain Room
Tel: 020 7734 8040
Afternoon tea at is served Mon–Sat between 3 and 5.30pm (£20–30; booking recommended).

Criterion Brasserie
224 Piccadilly, W1
Tel: (020) 7930 0488
Open: Mon–Sat noon–2.30pm and 6–11.30pm, Sun 6–10.30pm
Expensive
The food is excellent here and the room, all glamour and gold, is worth a visit for its own sake.

of rough wood he began to carry out his own experiments. From these humble beginnings he went on to became one of the greatest scientists of the 19th century, famous for a wide range of achievements, notably the invention of the first electric motor and dynamo. The museum includes parts of his original laboratory, which is in the basement of the Royal Institution.

Spencer House (7 mins)

27 St James's Place, SW1
***Tel**: (020) 7499 8620; www.spencerhouse.co.uk*
***Open**: Sun 10.30am–5.45pm (last adm 4.45pm), guided tours only (1 hr); closed Jan and Aug*
***Adm**: timed tickets, adults £6, concessions and children £5, no advance booking*

Spencer House was built in 1756–66 by the Palladian architect John Vardy for John Spencer, an ancestor of Diana, Princess of Wales, who became Earl Spencer in 1765. Generations of the Spencer family lived here until 1927, when the house was let to a succession of organisations including the Ladies Army and Navy Club and Christies.

From 1956 it was used as goverment offices, until its current owners purchased the lease in 1985; since then an extensive restoration has taken 10 years to bring the house back to its 18th-century splendour.

Highlights include the fantastical *Palm Room*, with columns disguised beneath carved and gilded palm trees, a frieze of griffins and candelabra, and a domed alcove; the richly ornamented ceiling of the *Great Room*; and the *Painted Room*, the first complete neoclassical interior in Europe

(finished in 1765) It is also famous for its décor on the theme of the Triumph of Love, reflecting the happy marriage of the then Lord and Lady Spencer.

⬤ VICTORIA

Royal Mews (5 mins)
Buckingham Palace Road, SW1
Tel: *(020) 7766 7302; www.royal.gov.uk*
Open: *Mar–end July and Oct, Sat–Thu 11am–4pm (last adm 3.15pm), end July–Sep daily 10am–5pm (last adm 4.15pm); closed 25 Mar, 28 May, 4 and 11 June and during state visits (call for info)*
Adm: *adults £6, children £3.50, concessions £5, family £15.50; Wheelchair accessible*

Children will love the Royal Mews for the glitter and chintz of the royal carriages kept here for state occasions. Among the many vehicles are Queen Victoria's Irish Coach, reserved for the state opening of Parliament, and the Glass State Coach, built in 1910, for royal weddings. The gilded State Coach, commissioned by George III, is for coronation ceremonies. The tiled stables for Her Majesty's Thoroughbred horses are also in the Mews; it takes eight of these mighty beasts, adorned with gleaming horse brasses, to pull the gold and jewel-encrusted State Coach.

Jenny Lo's Tea House
14 Eccleston Street, SW1

Tel: (020) 7259 0399

Open: Mon–Fri 11.30am–3pm, 6–10pm, Sat noon–3pm, 6–10pm

Moderate

Unfussy noodle bar; try the gunpowder and fresh mint tea.

Seafresh
80–81 Wilton Rd, SW1

Tel: (020) 7828 0747

Open: Mon–Sat noon–10pm

Moderate

Huge portions of excellent fish and chips in a restaurant behind Victoria station, cheerfully decorated with nets and shells. Grilled fish also available.

Chimes of Pimlico

26 Churton Street, SW1

Tel: (020) 7821 7456

Open: daily noon–3pm, 6–10.15pm

Moderate

A little way from the Cathedral. Wonderfully old-fashioned, authentic British food.

Westminster Cathedral (8 mins)

Victoria Street, SW1

Tel: (020) 7798 9055; www.westminstercathedral.org.uk

Open: Mon–Fri 7am–7pm, Sat–Sun 8am–7.30pm/5.30pm on bank or public hols

Adm: free; Wheelchair accessible

Westminster Cathedral, the premier place of worship for British Roman Catholics, was completed in 1903 although some of the decoration work on the interior has still to be completed. The neo-Byzantine excess of architect John Francis Bentley make this immense building hard to miss. And nor would you want to. The green marble columns (cut from the same stone as Istanbul's 6th-century St Sophia), the mosaics (fashioned from over 100 different kinds of marble) and Eric Gill's much admired statues of the 14 Stations of the Cross (1914–18) are all worthy of note. So, too is the organ, which is unique in Britain for having a dual control system, allowing it to be played from either end of the cathedral.

Mosaics, Westminster Cathedral

See also Jubilee Line, p.90

Parliament Square p.90, Houses of Parliament p.90, St Margaret's Church p.92, Westminster Abbey p.92, Whitehall p.94, Cabinet War Rooms p.94, Banqueting House p.95, Horse Guards p.96

See also Circle Line, p.73

St James's Park p.73, Guards' Museum p.73, Buckingham Palace p.74, Queens's Gallery p.76

PIMLICO

Tate Britain (8 mins)

Millbank, SW1
***Tel**: (020) 7887 8008; www.tate.org.uk*
***Adm**: daily 10am–5.50pm (exhibitions open 10am–5.40pm, last adm 5pm)*
***Adm**: free, but donations welcomed*
Gift shop, café and restaurant
Wheelchair accessible (entrance via Atterbury St)

The Tate Gallery, opened in 1897, was funded by Sir Henry Tate whose fortune was secure when he purchased the patent for a device that could manufacture sugar lumps. For years, all but 15 per cent of this national collection was locked away in vaults but, thanks to the opening of Tate Modern (*see* p.97), the space problem has largely been resolved. With a new-found purpose, the Tate Gallery has been given a new name and been freed up to devote itself solely to British art. For the first time in many years it is often comparatively quiet as most of the crowds have gone to Tate Modern. The collection is organized chronologically, divided into works from 1500 to 1900, and 1900 to now. Displays include pieces by the visionary artist William Blake, as well as Canaletto's glittering *View of London* (1749), famous Pre-Raphaelite works such as Sir John Everett Millais' *Ophelia* (1851–2) and *The Lady of Shalott* (1888) by John William Waterhouse.

Although there are Constables and Gainsboroughs aplenty to admire, it is well worth saving enough energy for the Clore Gallery extension, which houses a vast collection of paintings by J.M.W. Turner. It is

Shepherd's

Marsham Court, Marsham Street, SW1

Tel: (020) 7834 9552

Open: Mon–Fri noon–3pm, 6.30–11pm

Expensive

Food for discerning palates – a reasonably priced menu with seasonal specials. It's a stone's throw from the Houses of Parliament, and therefore the private booths are popular with MPs and journalists.

Entrance to Tate Britain

difficult, now, to appreciate now just how influential this son of a London barber was, yet his freedom in capturing effects of weather and light, in works such as *Steamer in a Snowstorm* (1842), predates Impressionism by over 30 years.

Among the later works, be sure not to miss Stanley Spencer's wonderful depiction *St Francis and the Birds* (1935), L.S. Lowry's bleak *Industrial Landscape* (1955), Jonathan Leaman's fun, Dutch-inspired *A Jan Steen Kitchen* (1995–6) or Peter Blake's *Self-Portrait with Badges* (1961). There are also works by Wyndham Lewis, Victor Passmore, Henry Moore and Ben Nicholson, plus rooms devoted to Patrick Caulfield, John Piper, Francis Bacon, Vanessa Bell and Antony Gormley and – how could we forget her? – Tracey Emin.

As before, there are plenty of things for children to do in the gallery. The ever-popular Art Trolley is wheeled out on Sundays between noon and 5pm and every day during the holidays, while the new Tate Trails, with a variety of drawing and looking activities, offer kids a fun way to explore the museum on their own.

Hampstead Village

FURTHER AFIELD

This book covers the central, zone 1 area of London, but London's Underground covers 253 miles and extends well beyond the centre of town. Staying on the Tube barely another 10–20 minutes will take you to leafier areas, such as Hampstead and Kew, trendier areas such as Camden and places, such as Walthamstow and Southfields, that you might not expect to find on the tourist trail. Explore beyond the centre and you will soon realise how big and varied London really is.

DISTRICT LINE

Hammersmith
Direction: Richmond or Ealing Broadway

London Wetlands Centre
Queen Elizabeth's Walk, Barnes, SW13
***Tel**: (020) 8409 4400; www.wwt.org.uk*
***Open**: summer 9.30am–6pm (last adm 5pm);
winter 9.30am–5pm (last adm 4pm)*
***Adm**: adults £6.75, seniors £5.50, children £4,
family £17.50*
*Gift shop, café, Sunday Carvery (Sun noon–3pm),
art gallery; Wheelchair accessible*
*15 mins' bus ride (take the 'Duck Bus', no.283,
from Hammersmith bus station – above and
right next to the tube station, from bus stop C
directly to the Centre)*

Created in 2000, this fascinating centre offers
100 acres of lakes, ponds and marshes full
of wetland life right next to the Thames.
There are lots of hands-on, interactive displays,
over two miles of footpaths, with hides,
bridges and viewing platforms and 14 global
wetland environments, each with appropriate
birdlife. In the *Pond Zone* you even can try
to catch pond creatures with your bare hands!

Kew Gardens
Direction: Richmond

Royal Botanic Gardens (5 mins)
Victoria Gate, Kew Road
***Tel**: (020) 8332 5655; www.rbgkew.org.uk*
***Open**: Gardens, daily 9.30am–dusk*
*Glasshouses and other buildings: daily
9.30am–5.30pm, Oct–Feb until 3.45pm*
*Climbers and Creepers Play Zone open, daily,
mid-Feb–Mar 10.30am–5pm, Apr–Oct
10.30am–5.30pm, Nov–Feb 10.30am–3.45pm*
***Adm**: adults £8.50, concessions £6/free,
under-16s free*
***Guided tours**: daily, 11am and 2pm (1 hour, free)*
Gift shops, 3 restaurants, café
*Wheelchair accessible; wear sturdy shoes if you
are likely to wander off the paths*

Kew Gardens was designated a World
Heritage Site in 2003. There's lots to see but
don't miss the *Palm House* (1844–8), full of
rainforest plants – several of which are

extinct in the wild; the *Temperate House* (1860–99), the world's largest ornamental glasshouse and home to the world's largest indoor plant; the *Waterlily House* (1851) built to house the giant water lily, whose leaves grow to a diameter of 2.5m (8ft); and the *Princess of Wales Conservatory*, which has 10 climactic zones, a wonderful display of orchids and tanks that contain leaf-cutter ants and poison-dart frogs.

In the gardens, there is a 10-storey Chinese-style pagoda (1761–2); the *Queen's Cottage* (1771) (open May bank holiday and most weekends July–Aug 10am–4pm); a Japanese *kaiyu shiki* ('stroll around') 16th-century style garden; *Kew Palace*, built in Dutch style and home to 'mad' King George III (closed for restoration in 2005); and *Queen Charlotte's Garden*, laid out in formal 17th-century style. Finally, there is the '*Climbers and Creepers*' play area where kids can climb into giant plants to 'pollinate' them or get 'eaten'.

Southfields

Direction: Wimbledon

Wimbledon Lawn Tennis Museum (15 mins)

All England Lawn Tennis and Croquet Club, Church Road, Wimbledon SW19
***Tel**: (020) 8946 6131*
***Open**: daily 10.30am–5pm, until 8pm or close of play during Championships; closed middle Sun and following Mon of Championships*
***Adm**: adults £6, concessions £5, under-16s £3.75, under-5s free*
***Guided tours**: Easter–end Oct daily, except during Championships, weekends only in winter (extra £7.25 charge)*
Gift shop, café; Wheelchair accessible
Bus no.493 (5 mins) leaves from near the station

This museum, located on the east side of Centre Court, details the development of tennis from medieval times, including a reconstruction of a gents' changing room from 1900, an exhibit on making tennis balls, Championship trophies and memorabilia from tennis players such as Björn Borg,

Café Centre Court

All England Lawn Tennis and Croquet Club

Tel: (020) 8946 6131

Inexpensive–Moderate

Serves breakfast, lunch and afternoon tea – including strawberries and cream.

Delicious Deli

308 Replingham Road, Southfields, SW18

Tel: (020) 8874 2138

Inexpensive

Open: Mon–Fri 8.30am–8pm, Sat 9am–5.30pm, Sun 9am–2pm

A deli that lives up to is name. There is a small café and garden (in summer) at the back.

Martina Navratilova, Tim Henman, Pat Cash, Todd Woodbridge and Mark Woodforde. Archive film and a costume gallery document tennis outfits and there is a small art gallery. The best bit is a behind-the-scenes tour to Court No.1 and the International Box in Centre Court.

JUBILEE LINE

⬤ Finchley Road

Freud Museum (6 mins)
20 Maresfield Gardens
Tel: *(020) 7435 2002; www.freud.org.uk*
Open: *Wed–Sun noon–5pm*
Adm: *adults £5, concessions and over 12s £3*
Gift shop; Wheelchair accessible

Sigmund Freud and his family lived here after they fled Vienna in 1938 during the Nazi invasion of Austria. Now an evocative museum, it celebrates the work and life of the founder of psychoanalysis and also his eminent daughter Anna, a pioneer in psycho-analytic work with children. The museum's natural focus is her father's opulent study and library, complete with his famous psychoanalytic couch, theatrically draped with a marvellous Iranian rug.

⬤ Canary Wharf

Museum in Docklands (9 mins)
West India Quay
Tel: *0870 444 3857;*
www.museumindocklands.org.uk
Open: *daily 10am–6pm, Wed until 8pm*
Adm: *adults £5, concessions £3, students and under-16s free*
Shop, café, restaurant; Wheelchair accessible

Housed in an 18th-century warehouse, this museum charts the history of London's docks. Inside, there are 12 galleries including the *Trade and Expansion gallery*, which explores trade from the 16th to 18th centuries; *Sailortown*, a re-creation of an early Victorian riverside; and *Docklands at War*, which shows the role of the docks during World War II, all using multimedia presentations.

Noodle Zone
634 Finchley Road, NW11
Tel: (020) 8458 2012
Open: Mon–Sat
noon–11..30pm, Sun
11am–11pm
Inexpensive
Healthy fast food, offering generous portions of soup, meat, rice and noodle dishes.

Itsu
Level 2, Cabot Place East, E14
Tel: (020) 7512 5790
Moderate
A Japanese sushi restaurant where dishes are sent out from the kitchen on a conveyor belt, and glide tantalizingly past your nose. Prices are classed by the colour of each dish's rim (gold is the most expensive; white the cheapest). Full marks for fun and flavour.

Amerigo Vespucci

25 Cabot Square, E14

Tel: (020) 7513 0288

Expensive

Classy Italian restaurant, with attentive service and an excellent menu.

In the *Children's Gallery* (5–11s), kids can winch, weigh and balance cargoes, construct Canary Wharf, or unearth archaeological objects in the Foreshore Discovery Box.

NORTHERN LINE

Camden Town

This station gets very overcrowed at peak times; entry from the street is prohibited on Sun afternoons; to re-enter the Tube after your visit, walk up Chalk Farm Road (the continuation of Camden High St) to Chalk Farm station, 5 mins from Camden Lock

Jamon Jamon

38 Parkway, NW1

Tel: (020) 7284 0606

Moderate

Fabulous Spanish tapas bar serving a range of dishes, from calamari to patatas bravas to Serrano ham.

Strada

40–42 Parkway, NW1

Tel: (020) 7428 9653; www.strada.co.uk

Moderate

A marvellous Italian menu; pizzas are cooked using a traditional wood-fired oven.

Camden Markets (3–7 mins)

Off Camden High Street
www.camdenlock.net
***Open**: daily 9.30am–6pm*
Lock and Stables markets wheelchair accessible

Camden's markets are the place for thrift-shopping, vintage clothes, collectables, rare LPs, furniture, crafts, Indian textiles... . The best place to start is just over the canal bridge. To your left are the *Camden Lock* buildings where you'll find a vast range of goods and services, from palmistry to clothes designers and books. Further on is the *Stable Market* – the place for furniture, vintage clothing and 20th-century antiques and collectables. If you are hungry, there is lots of takeaway food and outdoor seating.

Jewish Museum (4 mins)

129–131 Albert Street, NW1
***Tel**: (020) 7284 1997*
www.jewishmuseum.org.uk
***Open**: Mon–Thu 10am–4pm, Sun 10am–5pm (last adm 30 mins before close); closed Jewish festivals, 25–26 Dec and 1 Jan*
***Adm**: adults £3.50, seniors £2.50, concessions £1.50, family £8; Wheelchair accessible*

Located not far from the High Street, this modern exhibition space charts the history of Jewish culture and religion in Britain. It has a remarkable collection of ceremonial art, such as Passover plates, old English Hanukkah lamps and some fine embroidered textiles. The highlight is a magnificent 17th-century Venetian synagogue ark, which was found in use as a wardrobe at Chillingham Castle, Northumbria, in the 1930s.

Hampstead

Direction: Edgware

Hampstead Village (0 mins)

A pretty, one-time country village, Hampstead still fits its description from 1814 as 'a select, amicable, respectable and opulent neighbour-hood'. It became popular in the 1700s with the craze for medicinal spas and spring water, which is reflected in the street and pub names, such as Flask Walk and Well Walk with its pump room and baths. Over the last 300 years many famous people, Keats (*see* below), Byron, Constable, Anna Pavlova, Sigmund Freud (*see* p.180) and Katherine Mansfield, to name a few, have all lived here. Today it is home to superior clothes shopping, with names such as Nicole Farhi, Ronit Zilkha, and Agnes B, as well as many top-end chains.

Willow Road (8 mins)

2 Willow Road, NW3
Tel: *(020) 7435 6166; www.nationaltrust.org.uk*
Open: *Mar and Nov Sat noon–5pm, Apr–Oct Thu–Sat noon–5pm*
Adm: *adults £4.60, children £2.30, family £11.50*
Guided tours: *12, 1 and 2pm*
Wheelchair access to some public areas

This Modernist house (1937) was designed and built by architect Ernö Goldfinger as his family home (which it remained until 1994), and is one of the UK's most important examples of the period. Goldfinger also designed much of the furniture in the sleek and minimal interior, which is accompanied by important examples of art by Bridget Riley, Henry Moore, Marcel Duchamp and Max Ernst. One-time neighbour Ian Fleming so disliked Goldfinger that he named a villain after him in one of his James Bond novels; furious, Goldfinger made moves to sue (Fleming, equally livid, threatened to

The Coffee Cup

74 Hampstead High Street, NW3

Tel: (020) 7435 7565

Inexpensive

Snug, wood-panelled and slightly worn, the Coffee Cup has been here for years. Although the food isn't great it's a favourite spot for watching life go by over a hot drink.

The Holly Bush

22 Holly Mount, NW3

Tel: (020) 7435 2892

Moderate

Charming 17th-century pub tucked away from Hampstead's main drag, with simple decor: wooden floors, panelling and settles, with an open fire. Food is excellent

Giraffe

46 Rosslyn Hill, NW3

Tel: (020) 7435 0343

Moderate

One of a chain selling healthy world food in a fun setting.

Marine Ices

8 Haverstock Hill, NW3 (close to Chalk Farm tube)

Tel: (020) 7482 9003

Moderate

Authentic Italian ice-cream parlour and restaurant It's legendary for those who grew up in the area. The delicious ice cream is freshly made and restaurant portions are generous.

change the name to a lower part of the male anatomy) but a settlement was made. A copy of the book sits in the house today.

Keats' House Museum (12 mins)
Wentworth Place, Keats Grove, NW3
Tel: *(020) 7435 2062; www.cityoflondon.gov.uk*
Open: *Tue–Sun and bank hols 1–5pm*
Adm: *adults £3, concessions £1.50, children free*
Wheelchair access to some public areas
Note: there are plans to work on the interior during 2005–6; call before visiting

The Romantic poet John Keats lived in this leafy suburb during the last two years of his life before he died in Rome in 1820, aged 25.

He fell in love with his neighbour Fanny Brawne here and wrote a lot of poetry, including the famous *Ode to a Nightingale*, which, it is said, was written under the plum tree in the garden (the current one is not the original). Inside, the small museum displays some memorabilia, including a lock of Keats' hair, and some original notebooks and manuscripts; as well as related paintings, letters and prints. There's also a display on Fanny Brawne.

Freemasons Arms

32 Downshire Hill, NW3

Tel: (020) 7433 6811

Inexpensive

Located a stone's throw from the Heath, with a lovely garden, decent pub food and friendly service.

Hampstead Heath (12 mins)
www.cityoflondon.gov.uk
Turn left out of the station, left into Flask Walk, which becomes Well Walk, and keep walking.

On summer days, Londoners relax here, picnicking , flying kites on Parliament Hill (where there's a great view of the city); or swimming in one of the three freshwater ponds (there are separate Men's and Ladies' Ponds on the east side). Refreshments, playgrounds and outdoor sports are mainly in the southeast corner. It's a pleasant walk from Hampstead to Highgate (or vice versa), taking in Kenwood House (*see* below) along the way.

Kenwood House (34 mins)
Hampstead Lane, NW3
Tel: *(020) 8348 1286; www.english-heritage.org.uk www.picnicconcerts.com*
Open: *Apr–Oct daily 10am–5pm, Nov–Mar*

daily 10am–4pm (Wed and Fri house opens at 10.30am; grounds close before dusk, check signposts at its entrances)
Adm: *by donation*
Café, gift shop; Mainly wheelchair accessible
No. 210 bus from Archway station, 22 mins

This grand neoclassical house sits on a hill overlooking a lake and was designed by Robert Adam in 1754. It holds an important collection of paintings, including works by Rembrandt, Vermeer, Turner, Reynolds, Van Dyck, Gainsborough and William Larking. The main draw of the interior is the library, with a curved ceiling, gilding and panel paintings, and fluted Corinthian columns. In summer, evening picnic concerts are held here. In the rest of the grounds, which adjoin Hampstead Heath, there are sculptures by Barbara Hepworth and Henry Moore.

⭘ Archway
Direction: High Barnet

Highgate Hill (0 mins)

Turn left out of the station and a little way up the hill you will see the **Whittington Stone**, where Dick Whittington is said to have paused on hearing Bow bells (*see* p.64) as they let out a peal that seemed to sing: 'Turn again, Whittington, three times Lord Mayor of London'. Richard Whittington, son of a Gloucestershire landowner, was actually elected Lord Mayor four times, and the charitable trust he created in the 15th century is still benefiting people today.

Highgate Cemetery (13 mins)
Swain's Lane, Highgate, N6
Tel: *(020) 8340 1834*
www.highgate-cemetery.org
Open: *East Cemetery, Apr–Oct Mon–Fri 10am–4.30pm, Sat–Sun 11am–4.30pm; Nov–Mar Mon–Fri 10am–3.30pm, Sat–Sun 11am–3.30pm; West Cemetery, guided tours only, Mon–Fri at 2pm (1 hr; booking advised)*
Adm: *East Cemetery £2; West Cemetery £3; camera permits £1; No children under 8 yrs*

Over 850 famous people are buried in this cemetery, which is said to have the best

Brew House Café

Kenwood House, Hampstead Lane, NW3

Tel: (020) 8341 5384

Inexpensive

A great place for superior snacks, sandwiches and cakes, with a large, civilized garden seating area. It gets very busy at weekends.

Victorian funerary architecture in the UK. The West Cemetery, consecrated in 1839, is the oldest part. Look out for the sleeping lion on the grave of George Wombwell who bred the first lion in captivity, the Egyptian Avenue and the Circle of Lebanon, whose iron doors are decorated with inverted torches symbolizing death. In the East Cemetery, although the memorials are less impressive, are the graves, among others, of novelist George Eliot (real name Mary Ann Evans), Karl Marx, Michael Faraday (inventor of the electromagnet), Shakespearean actor Sir Ralph Richardson, sculptor Henry Moore, poet Christina Rossetti and Elizabeth Siddal, muse and wife of Pre-Raphaelite painter and poet Dante Gabriel Rossetti whose body he later exhumed in order to retrieve and publish the book of handwritten poetry that he had placed beside her.

VICTORIA LINE

Walthamstow Central

William Morris Gallery (15 mins)
Water House, Lloyd Park, Forest Road, E17
Tel: *(020) 8527 3782; www.lbwf.gov.uk/wmg*
Open: *Tue–Sat and first Sun of month 10am–1pm, 2–5pm*
Adm: *by donation*
Gift shop; Wheelchair access to the ground floor

This house, is the childhood home (1848–56) of William Morris, founder of the Arts and Crafts movement. The collection includes furniture, carpets, wallpapers, tapestries and stained glass designed by Morris, including the original design for an early wallpaper, 'Trellis', and the 'Labours of the Months' tile panels.

Also on show are designs by Edward Burne-Jones, Dante Gabriel Rossetti and Ford Madox Brown, several of Morris's colleagues. There are pieces by Morris's contemporaries, including tiles and ceramics by William de Morgan, furniture by Ernest Gimson and C.F.A. Voysey, glass by Harry Powel and paintings by Frank Brangwyn.

Manze's Pie and Mash Shop

76 Walthamstow High Street, E17

Tel: (020) 8520 2855; www.manze.co.uk

Open: Mon–Wed 10am–4pm, Thurs–Sat 10am–5pm

Inexpensive

This is the place for an authentic Cockney experience: a meat pie with a dollop of creamy mashed potato, accompanied by liquor (smooth parsley sauce, not alcohol), or jellied or hot eels. This shop has been here since 1929 and after a recent restoration still retains its charm, with black-and-white tiled floors, a long counter, seating booths and pretty tiles.

PRACTICAL INFORMATION

Finding somewhere to stay

There are lots of options in London for finding a hotel, a B&B (bed and breakfast), staying with a family or renting a short-let apartment. These are some useful resources.

The London Tourist Board

www.uk.visitlondon.com
Tel: 0845 644 3010
The Tourist Board runs a service dealing with every type of accommodation from hostels and B&Bs to upmarket hotels.

Youth Hostel Association

www.yha.org.uk
Tel: (020) 7373 3400

Host and Guest service

103 Dawes Road SW6
www.host-guest.co.uk
Tel: (020) 7385 9922

Late booking

Booking through the internet on a last-minute deal can give you some very good discounts, especially in central London business hotels at the weekends. Even if you book ahead, some hotels offer discounts for web bookings. These websites are useful.
www.laterooms.com
www.londontoolkit.com
www.lastminute.com
www.last-minute.hotels-london.co.uk
www.expedia.co.uk
www.direct-hotels.com
www.londonhotels.net

Tourist Information

Britain and London Visitor Centre

1 Regent Street, Piccadilly Circus, SW1
***Open**: Mon–Fri 9–6.30, Sat–Sun 10–4*

There are also tourist offices at Waterloo International terminal, Liverpool Street Station and Victoria Station.

Entertainment

The best source of information for what's on in London, from clubs to restaurants, cinemas, concerts and theatre are the daily papers and weekly entertainment magazines. Check out *Time Out*, London's best-selling weekly listings magazine for the most comprehensive listings or, if you pick it up on the right day, the *Evening Standard* does a listings magazine *Metro Life* every Thursday, the *Guardian* listings, *The Guide* comes out on Saturday and *The Times* and *The Independent* have listings on Sundays.

Smart restaurants will usually need to be booked. Ask about pre- and post-theatre supper and Sunday lunch fixed-price menus, which are usually very good value. For theatre tickets, ring venues direct to book or ask about standby availability (last-minute tickets one hour before the performance) and check out the official half-price ticket booth at the bottom of Leicester Square (open Mon–Sat 10am–7pm, Sun 12pm–3pm).

Also check out:
www.officiallondontheatre.co.uk
www.whatsonstage.com
www.viewlondon.co.uk
www.toptable.co.uk
www.hardens.com

Opening hours
Shops are usually open 9.30am–5.30pm although in some areas, such as Covent Garden, they may not open until 10am. Some also close later and Thursday is usually late-night shopping until 8pm/9pm. Some shops open on Sunday, usually 12 noon–5pm. Some corner shops and supermarkets stay open 24-hours.

Useful numbers
Emergency (Police, Fire Brigade, Ambulance) *Tel*: 999/112
Dental Emergency Care Service *Tel*: (020) 7955 2186; www.bda-findadentist.org.uk
Operator *Tel*: 100
Directory Enquiries *Tel*: 118500/118800/118118
International Operator *Tel*: 155
International Directory Enquiries *Tel*:153

INDEX